PRAISE FOR

Daily Steps for GodChicks®

Well, here you have it—a daily "get your hands around it Word made flesh" for GodChicks everywhere. You will enjoy Holly's personal and authentic style as she walks with you on your journey to beauty, power and purpose in God. It's never been so simple, yet so profound.

Lisa Bevere
Speaker and Author, *Fight Like a Girl* and *Kissed the Girls and Made Them Cry*

Spending daily time with our Creator is vital. In this devotional, Holly does a great job in helping us enter into that place of daily intimacy with God.

Christine Caine
Director, Equip and Empower Ministries

Holly, in her real, down-to-earth and completely delightful way, carries a depth that relates to women of all ages. I am confident that this daily devotional will encourage, inspire and point you in the direction of your true potential. Be blessed as you start the day with Jesus and one of my most treasured and loved girlfriends.

Bobbie Houston
Senior Pastor, Hillsong Church

Daily Steps for
God
Chicks

Holly Wagner

Regal

From Gospel Light
Ventura, California, U.S.A.

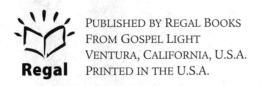

PUBLISHED BY REGAL BOOKS
FROM GOSPEL LIGHT
VENTURA, CALIFORNIA, U.S.A.
PRINTED IN THE U.S.A.

Regal Books is a ministry of Gospel Light, a Christian publisher dedicated to serving the local church. We believe God's vision for Gospel Light is to provide church leaders with biblical, user-friendly materials that will help them evangelize, disciple and minister to children, youth and families.

It is our prayer that this Regal book will help you discover biblical truth for your own life and help you meet the needs of others. May God richly bless you.

For a free catalog of resources from Regal Books/Gospel Light, please call your Christian supplier or contact us at 1-800-4-GOSPEL or www.regalbooks.com.

Scripture quotations are taken from the following versions:

AMP–Scripture taken from THE AMPLIFIED BIBLE, Old Testament copyright © 1965, 1987 by the Zondervan Corporation. The Amplified New Testament copyright © 1958, 1987 by The Lockman Foundation. Used by permission.
CEV–*Contemporary English Version*. Copyright © American Bible Society, 1995.
THE MESSAGE–Scripture taken from *THE MESSAGE*. Copyright © by Eugene H. Peterson, 1993, 1994, 1995. Used by permission of NavPress Publishing Group.
NCV–Scriptures quoted from *The Holy Bible, New Century Version*, copyright © 1987, 1988, 1991 by Word Publishing, Nashville, Tennessee. Used by permission.
NIV–Scripture taken from the *Holy Bible, New International Version®*. Copyright © 1973, 1978, 1984 by International Bible Society. Used by permission of Zondervan Publishing House. All rights reserved.
NKJV–Scripture taken from the *New King James Version*. Copyright © 1979, 1980, 1982 by Thomas Nelson, Inc. Used by permission. All rights reserved.
NLT–Scripture quotations marked *(NLT)* are taken from the *Holy Bible*, New Living Translation, copyright © 1996. Used by permission of Tyndale House Publishers, Inc., Wheaton, Illinois 60189. All rights reserved.

All citations for defined words are from the *American Heritage® Dictionary of the English Language*, Fourth Edition (Boston, MA: Houghton Mifflin Company, 2000).

Cover Illustration by Curt Dawson
Interior Photos by Edward Duarte

Library of Congress Cataloging-in-Publication Data
Wagner, Holly.
  Daily steps for GodChicks / Holly Wagner.
     p. cm.
  ISBN 0-8307-3930-0 (hard cover)
  1. Christian women—Religious life. 2. Devotional calendars. I. Title.
BV4527.W296 2006
242'.643—dc22   2005037157

11 12 13 14 15 16 17 / 15 14 13 12 11 10 09

Rights for publishing this book in other languages are contracted by Gospel Light Worldwide, the international nonprofit ministry of Gospel Light. Gospel Light Worldwide also provides publishing and technical assistance to international publishers dedicated to producing Sunday School and Vacation Bible School curricula and books in the languages of the world. For additional information, visit www.gospellightworldwide.org; write to Gospel Light Worldwide, P.O. Box 3875, Ventura, CA 93006; or send an e-mail to info@gospellightworldwide.org.

Dedication

This book is for all of you GodChicks who are
committed to the daily journey of walking with
God. I am honored to be on the planet at
the same time you are!

Contents

Introduction

Honestly, this year has been the most challenging one in my life. I have had to remind myself about a thousand times that what won't kill me will make me stronger! Maybe you have had a year like that . . . or a month like that . . . or even a day like that!

There were so many days during the past few months when I truly came to the end of myself . . . when my strength vanished and I had to reach for the much greater strength of my God. Not a bad thing to do, really!

I was diagnosed with breast cancer earlier this year and have been on a healing journey ever since. As you might expect, the initial diagnosis was a total shock. "Cancer" is a scary word to have spoken over your life. But I have made many changes as a result of the diagnosis—most of them good ones! (I eat a lot more green stuff now!)

One of the best things I did was to be very diligent about spending time every day with God. I have been following Christ for more than 20 years, so I certainly know the importance of taking time to read the Bible and pray. It is just that this year, the quiet, still time I spent in the morning became my salvation. I truly hungered for my time with God. It became more than just my Christian duty . . . it was my lifeline.

I use different devotionals to help me during my time with God. Most offer a simple thought and a verse that basically allows me to focus my time. Because of how much these devotionals have helped me, I wanted to write one that would help other women.

Daily Steps for GodChicks is filled with 90 days of devotionals. For those of you who are new at using a devotional, I think 3 months is a good length of time to develop a habit of spending quiet time with God . . . for those of you who are old pros at using devotionals, enjoy these 3 months! There is no wrong way to use this book.

The first 10 days are filled with general thoughts to help guide you in your time with your Father. The other 80 days are geared more specifically toward developing the different aspects of the GodChick within you. Hopefully these thoughts will then trigger your own study.

My hope is that this book (along with your Bible, of course!) will help you navigate through some great moments with God. Actually, I commend you for picking up this devotional . . . and even more so for wanting to spend time with your God.

Maybe you have been facing a health challenge, financial problems, or perhaps a crisis in your family . . . or maybe you are having an awesome year! Regardless, every day will be better when you start it out with a few moments of building your relationship with your Creator.

GodChicks was my attempt to paint the picture of the awesome woman that you are and are becoming. My prayer is that this daily-step book will help you on your journey of becoming all that your Father had in mind when He created you!

So let's begin the adventure!

Holly Wagner
August 26, 2005

❀

Daily Steps for
God
Chicks

Day 1

*O LORD, hear me as I pray; pay attention to my
groaning. Listen to my cry for help, my King and my God,
for I will never pray to anyone but you. Listen to my
voice in the morning, LORD. Each morning I bring my
requests to you and wait expectantly.*

PSALM 5:1-3, *NLT*

I must confess . . . I am not usually a morning person. I like to
stay up late and then sleep in late . . . or at least as late as possible. Life has intruded on that little preference, however!
Children do not let us moms sleep late . . . and I guess we had
better get up and go to work!

I just wanted to make that point clear so that you would
understand just how unusual it has been for me to get up early
this past year and spend time with my God. Previously, I would
talk to God throughout the day, or at night . . . but this year
I have been the early bird. And I have *loved* it. It is now such a
habit that I can't imagine starting my day without a regular chat
with God. I even get a little annoyed if anything or anyone tries
to infringe on that time . . . whereas before, distractions—if not
exactly welcome—were certainly easy to go with!

I want to encourage you as you begin to spend these
moments with God. The point is that you spend time each day

with the Lord. Don't just rush through these moments . . . this is not a matter of clocking in and out or just doing your Christian duty. It is about developing a relationship with your loving Creator. He can't and won't ever force a relationship on you. He just longs for you to willingly love Him and choose to spend time with Him.

If I am going to have a great relationship with my husband, it will involve spending time with him . . . not time grudgingly given, but time freely and lovingly given . . . talking to him and, just as much (if not more), listening to him. (OK, that's the hard part!!)

As David cried in the psalm, "Hear me as I pray; . . . Listen to my voice in the morning . . . I bring my requests to you and wait expectantly." Your heavenly Father longs to deepen His relationship with you. He is waiting for you to come and talk to Him. Tell Him your fears . . . your dreams . . . your thoughts . . . your wants. He knows them anyway; He just wants to hear them from you!

Daily Step

Tell God your biggest fear and your biggest dream.

Don't fret or worry. Instead of worrying, pray. Let petitions and praises shape your worries into prayers, letting God know your concerns. Before you know it, a sense of God's wholeness, everything coming together for good, will come and settle you down. It's wonderful what happens when Christ displaces worry at the center of your life.

PHILIPPIANS 4:6-7, *THE MESSAGE*

There are moments when I could probably have been awarded a gold medal in worrying. It is five minutes past my son's curfew . . . where is he? What will the results of the surgery be? How should I handle that friend's betrayal? Will I have enough money for _____?

I would imagine that you have had gold-medal worry moments as well. The challenge is to turn your worries into prayers. I have found that if I pray about something, truly turning it over to God, a sense of wholeness does come and settle me down.

There was a man in the Old Testament named Jehoshaphat (some name, huh?). He found out that more than one army was coming to attack him and the children of Israel. He was just a *little* worried!! We all are when surrounded by enemies.

One of the first things Jehoshaphat did upon finding out about his enemies was to pray. He told God about the armies coming against him and said that he had no might to stand against them, but he knew that God did. He let God know that he was looking to Him for deliverance. And God did the coolest thing: He told Jehoshaphat that the upcoming battle was not Jehoshaphat's, but God's. God wanted Jehoshaphat and his boys to just take up their positions. God would do the fighting for them.

Jehoshaphat took the position of prayer and worship. As he exalted God, God fought the battle on his behalf.

There have been many days that I have been so worried about something as I sat down to have my time with God. But as I began to pray . . . to worship . . . to read His Word, something happened. Christ and His peace filled the place in which the worry had been. It will be the same for you.

Daily Step

On a sheet of paper, write down something that you are worrying about. Now, take that paper and hold it up as if you are offering it to God, and say something like this: "I let go of this worry, Father, trusting that You will take care of it." Now, throw that piece of paper in the trash. And don't take it out!! You have given it to your Father, and He is more than capable of handling it.

Day 3

*Devote yourselves to prayer with an alert
mind and a thankful heart.*

COLOSSIANS 4:2, *NLT*

---

de·vote *v:* to give or apply (one's time, attention, or self)
entirely to a particular activity, pursuit, cause, or person

This year I truly began to understand what it means to be devoted.

Certainly there were moments when I devoted myself to cancer research . . . and information on health. I have read so many health books that I feel like I should have a Ph.D. or something!! And throughout 20 years of marriage, I have been devoted to my husband . . . though probably more at some moments than others!

Devotion implies faithfulness and loyalty. At any moment of any day, you and I are devoted to something . . . friends, children, careers, dinner preparations, studying, working out—the list goes on.

When we devote ourselves to something, it consumes us. During the moments we spend with God, we should be totally devoted . . . giving ourselves entirely to the pursuit of building a relationship with our Creator. There are no set time guidelines, no timecard to punch in and out. Some days you might spend an hour with God, while other days just a few moments . . . remember, it is about the relationship. The goal is to deepen the relationship and hopefully to come out looking a little more like the woman God created you to be. How awesome that the God who created the universe wants to have an intimate relationship with us!

Prayer involves talking and listening. And, according to Paul, the basis of our prayers should be a grateful heart. Some days that is a challenge, because our need seems so large that it almost overshadows the gratitude. With the magnitude of the need, we can easily forget all of the things that we have to be thankful for. But you can't let it! God wants us to ask Him for help, provision, healing . . . whatever. He just wants us to do the asking with a grateful heart.

So many times I start my requests to God by saying, "Thank you, Father, that You have promised me health . . . or peace . . . or strength . . . or wisdom." Let's start our requests off with thanking Him for our family, our health, our friends, our jobs, our home in heaven . . . the list is endless. We have much to be grateful for.

Daily Step

Write down five things that you are thankful for . . . and then thank God for them . . . out loud.

Day 4

> *Worship the LORD with gladness; come before*
> *him with joyful songs.*

PSALM 100:2, *NIV*

Part of our time with God will include worship. Worship is expressing love to our God. This happens in a lot of ways . . . and it doesn't have to involve music (which is good news for those of us who can't sing a note!).

One way to worship God is to know who He is and to declare it. Getting to know God is the same as with any friend. In developing a relationship with someone, we get to know who that person is and what he or she is like. In getting to know one of my girlfriends, I learned that she is very patient (it takes that to be a friend of mine!!) and likes things peaceful. I did my best to accommodate her need for peace as we were developing a friendship. Another friend of mine loves to laugh. So do I . . . so I would find things for us to laugh about (often times it would be only the two of us laughing! ☺).

We get to know God by discovering who He is. And the Bible is full of descriptions of our awesome God! His name is equivalent to His presence. And God has quite a few names . . . *all* of which describe who He is.

When Jesus was teaching the disciples to pray, He began what is known as the Lord's Prayer (actually, I think it is more the "disciples prayer" than the Lord's Prayer!) with a declaration of worship: *Our Father, who is in heaven, hallowed be your name.*

In the book of Judges, Gideon, who was dealing with an inferiority complex, was given a great assignment from God. An angel appeared to Gideon and told him that God wanted Gideon to lead the children of Israel in a battle against the Midianites. Gideon did not see himself as a warrior. He complained that his clan was the weakest and that he was the least in his family. He was just a little freaked out! But God reassured him . . . and said, "Peace be with you; do not fear" (Judges 6:23, *NKJV*). Gideon immediately built an altar to the Lord and called it "The Lord is Peace."

There have been many times during this past year when I have had my own freak-out moments. Hearing the diagnosis of cancer was certainly one of those moments. Having to wait for test results was another. Trying to make the best health decisions was yet another. These were just a few of the times when I had to call on the God who is Peace . . . when I worshiped Him as my peace . . . when I thanked Jesus for the peace He left . . . when I worked hard not to let my heart be troubled. Maybe you are having one of those moments now.

Daily Step

*Right now . . . out loud . . .
thank God for being your peace.
Thank Him for bringing peace into
your marriage, your family,
your heart and your mind.*

Day 5

He [God] Himself has said, I will not in any way fail you nor give you up nor leave you without support. [I will] not, [I will] not, [I will] not in any degree leave you helpless nor forsake nor let [you] down (relax My hold on you)! [Assuredly not!]

HEBREWS 13:5, *AMP*

In the book of Ezekiel, we encounter the children of Israel, who were in despair because they had lost (or would soon lose) everything . . . their freedom, their country, their Temple and, for many, their lives. In the midst of this devastation, Ezekiel offered hope, showing them that God was at work. He ends his book by calling the new Jerusalem "The Lord is There."

What a great declaration of who God is . . . He is there! We do *not* serve a God who has abandoned us. His very name means that He is present.

Knowing that my God promised not to fail me in any way—or to leave me without support—was the most incredible support to me this past year. One day, I was in my hospital room and was slightly overwhelmed with a few of the treatments. OK . . . I was actually feeling just a bit sorry for myself! No one was with me and I was feeling very alone . . . and a little afraid.

Then I remembered the verse in Hebrews and I began to worship the God who is there. I began to thank Him for not leaving me helpless or forsaking me or relaxing His hold on me. I can't even describe the peace that came upon me as I realized that even though it looked like I was alone, I was not. The very God who created the universe was in that hospital room with me.

How awesome that we serve a God who never leaves us. He is with us through every good time and every bad time . . . every time of blessing and every time of loss. He is with us when we are afraid. He is with us when we are confused. He is always there. Period.

I am sure that you, like me, have felt alone at times. Maybe you feel alone even right now. Take a moment and call out to God who is there. Because He is.

Daily Step

Write down a time when you know God was there for you. And then lift your hands (really) and thank God that being there is who He is. Thank Him for being the God who is always present.

And be sure of this: I am with you always, even to the end of the age.

MATTHEW 28:20, NLT

Day 6

Every part of Scripture is God-breathed and useful one way or another—showing us truth, exposing our rebellion, correcting our mistakes, training us to live God's way. Through the Word we are put together and shaped up for the tasks God has for us.

2 TIMOTHY 3:16-17, *THE MESSAGE*

I love to read. My idea of a great vacation involves a beach and a good book or two . . . or 10! I read books that teach me, books that make me laugh, books that inspire me, books that trigger my imagination . . . and books that make me cry. I just love it when a book can take me outside of myself and bring me into a whole new world.

I enjoy talking to my friends about the books we are reading. In fact, just last night I spoke with a friend about a book that I had read quite a while ago, which I then recommended to her. We were such girls on the phone . . . both of us practically talking at the same time as we enthused over different parts of the book: "Did you cry at that part?" "Did the end surprise you?"

But for all the books I have read, there is no book that has shaped my life as much as the Bible. The interesting thing about the Bible is that while much of it contains stories about other people and other events, it is very personal. Too many people, perhaps, keep their Bible on a shelf and never open it to allow God to speak.

His Word is His voice. He longs for you and me to open it and become familiar with His voice. My time with God always involves reading His Word. As I read the Bible, it is almost as if God is inviting me into His very big world and opening up the possibility that His world can become my own. It is not a question of how much I read, but rather how I let His Word shape my day. Some days I read quite a few chapters, while other days it is just a few verses.

God will probably not speak to you in an audible voice or use skywriting or a message in a bottle to give you direction. He will speak to you through His Word.

His Word is your map for living. It is your GPS. It is your navigation system. When you are taking a road trip and plan on arriving at a specific destination, you probably don't just point your car in any direction and go. No, I imagine you have a plan. Well, God's Word is your plan for life. Without it, you will never arrive where you want to go. It is very easy to get lost on the highway of life . . . but not if you are using His Word as your guide.

Daily Step

Today, begin a Bible reading plan. (I have included one in the back of the book . . . or you can come up with your own.) Read a portion of God's Word and let it speak to you.

Day 7

Thank GOD because he's good, because his love never quits.
Tell the world, Israel, "His love never quits." And you, clan
of Aaron, tell the world, "His love never quits." And you
who fear GOD, join in, "His love never quits."

PSALM 118:1, *THE MESSAGE*

Over the years I have received quite a few love letters from my husband, Philip (what a guy!). In these letters, he describes his love for me, his thankfulness for our life, and his hopes for our future.

My heart is always softened when I read Philip's tender words of love. Sometimes, I even reread them if we are in the middle of not getting along. I remind myself of the truth of his love . . . especially during the times when I am not feeling it!

Well, you and I have another love letter to open. The Bible is God's love letter to you and me. Page after page reveals God's love for us. God is not mad at you! He loves you with a love that is beyond compare. You will discover His love as you read His Word.

God so greatly loved the world that He sent Jesus to pay the price of our failings (see John 3:16). God is love and there is nothing you and I can do that will separate us from His abiding, ever passionate love! (See 1 John 4:16; Romans 8:38.) The more

I read God's Word, the more convinced I am of His constant love for me.

As I read story after story after story of Jesus healing the sick, I felt loved and knew that His healing was available for me, too. I read that if He cares for the sparrows, He certainly cares for me (see Matthew 10:29). I read that God proves His love for me by the fact that while I was still a sinner, He offered His Son as a sacrifice (see Romans 5:8).

And His definition of love is not the definition the world uses. The love found in the world is perhaps temporal and easily offended . . . but not the love that our Father offers us.

His love never fails. His love is patient. His love is forgiving. His love is eternal. He will never stop loving you. Ever.

Daily Step

Say out loud, "I am loved by my Father in heaven with a love that is beyond compare. He will never stop loving me."

Day 8

Your word is a lamp to my feet and a light to my path.

PSALM 119:105, *AMP*

Earlier this year, I was training to walk in the Avon Walk for Breast Cancer. I would be walking a marathon, so my training walks were loooonnnnng! One particular evening, I was out walking on a trail not far from my house and it started to get dark. The trail was not lit, and I soon found myself tripping over tree roots, rocks . . . and my own feet! (Very graceful!) I was tripping over things that I would not have if the trail had been lit or I had walked on it during the day.

Many times in life, I have found myself stumbling over decisions because I have not let the Word of God bring in the light. His Word will light our path. Without the illumination of His Word, we can find ourselves tripping not so gracefully through life!

Not only is God's Word the greatest love letter ever, but it is also our instruction manual for living. Everything that we need to know about how to live a successful life is included in His Word.

God's Word is a lamp to our feet . . . which means that it provides illumination for the next step we must take. There are so many times on this journey of life that we just don't know the next thing we should do or the next decision we should make. That in itself can produce stress and anxiety. Life is full of questions.

I have found God's Word to be faithful at helping light the path in front of me . . . the path that I should take.

All along my healing journey, I have been faced with decisions, and each one brought a new level of concern. As I read my Bible, peace would enter my heart and the decision I needed to make seemed less difficult.

I have two teenagers . . . *yee hah!!* . . . and many times I am at a loss about how to parent them. But as I read God's Word and find scriptures about parenting, I find the answers I need. His Word does offer solutions. Our job is simply to find the answers as we read the Bible and then to do what it says.

Of course, this is easier said than done. Reading about forgiveness is easier than forgiving. Reading about loving our enemies is easier than doing it. Reading about loving God with our whole heart, soul and mind is easier than doing it.

But it starts with reading. Read His word. Do what it says. And watch your life change.

Daily Step

Find a Bible verse to help you with a situation that you are facing right now. (Maybe you can use one that I have included in the back.)

The entrance and unfolding of Your words give light; their unfolding gives understanding (discernment and comprehension) to the simple.

PSALM 119:130, *AMP*

Day 9

Dear friend, listen well to my words; tune your ears to my voice. Keep my message in plain view at all times. Concentrate! Learn it by heart! Those who discover these words live, really live; body and soul, they're bursting with health.

PROVERBS 4:20-23, *THE MESSAGE*

"Hey, Holly, watcha doing?"

That was all I had to hear to know exactly who was on the phone. I have a number of friends who don't have to tell me who they are when they call . . . I simply recognize their voice. Their voice is familiar to me because I have heard it hundreds of times. Some of them have very distinct accents, and some of them have very low voices. But regardless, I just know who it is.

One of my greatest desires is that I will become that familiar with the voice of my Father. I know that in order for that to happen, I must hear it over and over again. The way that we can *tune our ears to His voice* is to read His Word until it becomes familiar to us.

And the amazing thing is that listening to His words and learning them comes with a promise: *that we will live, really live, body and soul . . . we will be bursting with health.* My job is to hear and learn the truth of His Word . . . which sometimes can be different from the facts surrounding me.

The fact is that I was diagnosed with infiltrating ductal carcinoma. The truth is that Jesus was wounded so that I could be healed (see 1 Peter 2:24). The fact is that I was afraid. The truth is that His outstretched arms protect me so that I can fear nothing . . . not even disease. If I hold on to Him, He will get me out of trouble and give me a long life! (See Psalm 91.)

Reading God's Word is hearing His voice. The more we hear His voice, the more we become familiar with Him and can distinguish between the facts of our circumstance and the truth of His Word.

As the young shepherd David faced the Philistines, he heard the facts about his enemy, Goliath. Fact: Goliath was a giant . . . he would have made Shaquille O'Neal look puny. David was a youth. Fact: Goliath had top-notch weapons. David had a used slingshot. Fact: Goliath had years of military experience. David had never seen a battle before.

But all those facts paled next to the truth: David was loved and anointed by God for victory. As you read God's Word, you will discover that you are too.

Daily Step

Write down the facts about
a situation you are in and then
balance that with what the truth
of God's Word says about it.

Day 10

Are you tired? Worn out? Burned out on religion? Come to me. Get away with me and you'll recover your life. I'll show you how to take a real rest. Walk with me and work with me—watch how I do it. Learn the unforced rhythms of grace. I won't lay anything heavy or ill-fitting on you. Keep company with me and you'll learn to live freely and lightly.

MATTHEW 11:28-30, *THE MESSAGE*

Sometimes I feel as if I should join the circus. No, I can't tame elephants (although I can have a conversation with a teenage boy, so that's pretty close!!) and no, I can't contort my body to fit in a shoebox . . . but I am a champion plate spinner! I have so many plates spinning that I amaze myself. Can you relate? Probably. I have the woman plate going, the wife plate going, the mom plate going, the pastor plate going, the author plate going, the speaker plate going, and the friend plate going.

There are moments when I just feel a little worn out. Sometimes that realization hits me while standing in the shower (the only place I can find solitude some days!). Recently, I had to speak at a women's retreat, which means a weekend full of messages . . . in another state. I also had a book to finish (you are reading it!), my kid's basketball games to attend, GodChicks® Conference planning meetings, three Sunday services to get ready for, an annoying legal battle, a household to run, and I am sure my husband would like to eat and have sex somewhere in between. And, did I mention this was all during daily radiation treatments?? That's a lot of plates!

I have learned that the only way to negotiate all the plates that God has given me is to get great at walking with Jesus. When I spend my time with Him, everything else gets put in perspective. Instead of panicking at all that I need to accomplish today, I really am peaceful. In fact, many times I have gotten up from chatting with God and discovered the answers on how to fit all the pieces of my day together. By giving God that time, He has seemingly given me more.

Religion can be exhausting. There is no way that you and I can keep all the rules. And the enemy, like the Pharisees of the New Testament, wants us to feel guilty for not doing everything right. Jesus knew this, so He said that if we are burned out on religion, we just have to get away with Him. Only with Him can we learn *the unforced rhythms of grace.*

Rest in Him, my friend. Keep company with Him and you will live lighter than you ever have.

Daily Step

Just take a deep breath and let God's peace settle in you. For 60 seconds, just be still. Then ask God to direct your day.

Day 11

*I no longer call you servants, because a servant
does not know his master's business. Instead, I have called
you friends, for everything that I learned from my
Father I have made known to you.*

JOHN 15:15, *NIV*

---

friend *n:* a person whom one knows, likes, and trusts

ac·quain·tance *n:* knowledge of a person acquired by
a relationship less intimate than friendship

I know a lot of people. I would recognize the person who works at my dry cleaner, the grocery store clerk and the UPS man. These people are acquaintances. I smile at them and maybe have a short conversation. I also have friends . . . those people whom I know, like and trust.

Every friend that you and I have started off as an acquaintance. Nothing wrong with that. The first step in moving someone from being an acquaintance to being a friend is by spending more time with her. The time spent isn't regulated, but it is regular.

Some of my closest friends live on the other side of the planet, so we have gotten good at e-mailing and having phone conversations (my husband loves the phone bills!!). We also go out of our way to connect in person on a regular basis. When Philip and I first met, he was an acquaintance, someone my roommate knew. He kept coming around however, and soon we became friends . . . and then an even deeper relationship developed. ☺

In order for any relationship to develop, time has to be invested. How do we do that?

Well, we pray . . . we have a real conversation that involves talking and listening. We worship Him . . . we declare who He is: our God, our Protector, our Comforter, our Healer, our Peace and our Provider. We read His Word.

And like any friendship, the time is not forced . . . it is enjoyed. There is no pressure. So, relax, grab a cup of coffee . . . tea . . . carrot juice . . . whatever—and settle in to enjoy some time with your God, who wants to be your friend.

Daily Step

Pick a cozy spot and make it your regular place to meet with God.

Day 12

*And I praise you because of the wonderful way you
created me. Everything you do is marvelous! Of this I have
no doubt. With your own eyes you saw my body being
formed. Even before I was born, you had written
in your book everything I would do.*

PSALM 139:14, CEV

I love this verse. Can't you just see King David looking in the mirror and thanking God for the magnificent way he was made? While I do smile when I read it, it is a powerful truth. If more of us had a clear picture of how wonderfully we were made, then perhaps we would spend less time trying to be someone else.

I spent—or rather, wasted—quite a few years trying to be someone else. I looked at some other women who were teachers of the principles of God and thought that I should be like them. So I began to do my hair like them and dress like them. I even tried to talk like them. Really, it was pathetic.

Finally, I had a moment with God when He challenged me. I felt Him say to me, "Holly, those women are doing fine being who they are. I don't need you to be them. What I need is for you to become who it is I have called you to be." I was so grateful to hear these words from God that I quickly took off the conservative suits that my heroes wore and put on the funky clothes that I like to wear.

There is only one you. You are an absolute . . . one of a kind . . . unique creation of God Himself. No one else can do what He has called you to do. I wonder if we aren't slapping Him in the face when we desire to be anyone other than ourselves. You are giving your best when you are being *you*—not what you *think* people want you to be—but who you actually *are*.

You have got to get good at looking in the mirror and liking the girl you see. You are wonderfully made . . . never forget that! When God made you, He threw out the mold. He does not make mistakes. You are one of a kind, precious and priceless. Your worth is beyond compare.

So head on over to the mirror right now, look at your wonderfully unique face, and say, "Wow . . . thank You, God, for making me just the way You did!!" And if you are really feeling brave (or even if you're not!) give yourself a little whistle . . . go ahead!

Daily Step

*I wasn't kidding about the mirror
thing . . . go do it!*

Day 13

*I am your Creator. You were in my care even
before you were born. Israel, don't be terrified! You are
my chosen servant, my very favorite.*

ISAIAH 44:2, CEV

I love watching the track and field races during the Olympics. I used to especially enjoy watching Florence Griffith Joyner . . . I loved her very unconventional style!! The long hair, the flashy outfits, the long nails . . . and the fact that she was a winner. She was determined to be herself, and I think that this (along with a *lot* of training!) helped her capture four medals in the 1988 Olympic games.

One thing I notice about sprinters is that each of them must run in his or her own lane. In fact, the sprinters would get disqualified if they decided to try to run in someone else's lane. And yet I wonder, *How many of us are trying to get through life running in someone else's lane?* We are all supposed to do great things on the earth. And each of us is given different gifts and different tools with which to do those great things.

You were gifted and called by God to run in the lane that He set before you . . . not in my lane or the lane of your friend. Your gifts and talents won't help me to fulfill my purpose (other than be an inspiration to me) . . . and my gifts and talents won't help you.

I really love to sing. Unfortunately, no one (other than God ☺) really wants to hear me. There were times when I was convinced that God made a mistake and I was supposed to be a singer . . . and so I wasted many hours trying to pursue something that wasn't mine. I was looking at all of the lovely singer chicks and I wanted to run in their lane.

I was so busy trying to run in someone else's lane that I wasn't even focusing on what it was that God called me to do. What is the reason I am here?

We often spend irreplaceable time desiring what another woman has. It is because we misunderstand our own value that we find ourselves wanting someone else's. Oprah gives us a great reminder about the treasure inside of us: "You have a gift that only you can give the world—that's the whole reason you're on the planet. Use your precious energy to build a magnificent life that really is attainable. The miracle of your existence calls for celebration every day."[1]

It is good to be inspired by other runners, but remember to keep focused on the reason God created you. Dr. Martin Luther King, Jr., said, "Everyone has the power of greatness—not for fame but greatness, because greatness is determined by service." You are His chosen servant. It is your job to begin the adventure of figuring out in just what area you are to be His servant.

Daily Step

Write down three things you are great at . . . and one thing you are passionate about.

Day 14

*Before I formed you in the womb I knew and approved of
you [as My chosen instrument], and before you were born
I separated and set you apart, consecrating you; [and]
I appointed you as a prophet to the nations.*

JEREMIAH 1:5, *AMP*

---

con·se·crate *v:* to set apart for a high purpose

What an awesome thought! Before you even saw the light of day,
God knew all about you. He knew your strengths, your weaknesses, your potential and your personality. And He approved of
you. You don't have to earn His approval . . . you have had it
from before the time you were born.

Not only did God know you, but He also had great plans for
you. Not average mediocre plans . . . but *great* plans. He set you
apart for a high purpose. He had a path set out for you to discover and to walk.

So many children (and perhaps you too) have been taught
that they are basically just exploded tadpoles, randomly placed
on the earth with no particular purpose in mind. With this kind
of teaching out there, it is little wonder that many of us feel no
sense of purpose and don't truly value the life we have been given.

You were put on the planet on purpose. You are not some accident—no matter what people may have told you. There is something specific that you were created to do. When you discover your life mission, you will feel a sense of purpose and become confident in who you are.

Perhaps you feel as if your life . . . the life God designed for you . . . has been interrupted. Maybe something has knocked you off course . . . hurts, betrayal, sickness. Let me tell you: It is never too late to start again. It is never too late to get back in the lane God designed for you. He is the restorer. He is the God of the second, third and thousandth chance.

Your life has value. The sooner you realize that, the sooner you can make a difference in your world. And that is why we were all created—to make a difference. We will each do it in a different way . . . but we will all make a difference.

Portraying William Wallace in the movie *Braveheart*, Mel Gibson said, "Every man dies, but not every man really lives." Make this a day that you really live!

Daily Step

Describe to a friend the lane that you have been assigned to run in.

Day 15

> *God isn't late with his promise as some measure lateness.*
> *He is restraining himself on account of you, holding back*
> *the End because he doesn't want anyone lost. He's giving*
> *everyone space and time to change.*

2 PETER 3:9, THE MESSAGE

Have you ever been impatient? OK . . . that was a stupid question! When was the last time you felt that you were doing a lot of waiting??

I am waiting for the day my son will leap up from the table and say, "Mom, why don't you sit on the couch and I will clean the kitchen." I am waiting for my husband to give me the remote control and say, "We'll watch whatever you want to watch, honey." I am waiting for there to be no traffic on the freeway between my home and the office. I am waiting for chocolate brownies to be good for me . . . and the list continues.

Second Peter 3:8-9 tells us, "With God, one day is as good as a thousand years, a thousand years as a day. God isn't late with his promises as some measure lateness." *Well, sometimes He is,* I often think to myself . . . *at least according to my schedule.* Don't you often feel the same?

In fact, God is never late. He is also never early. We might feel as if we have been waiting forever, but He fulfills His promises (not necessarily our nonsensical dreams!) right on time.

Right now I am waiting for full evidence of my healing from breast cancer. God has promised us health, so I know that I can count on Him to fulfill that promise: "If you listen, listen obediently to how God tells you to live in his presence, obeying his commandments and keeping all his laws, then I won't strike you with all the diseases . . . I am God your healer" (Exodus 15:26, *THE MESSAGE*).

He has promised that He will continue and finish the work He began in you: "God is the one who began this good work in you, and I am certain the he won't stop before it is complete on the day that Christ Jesus returns" (Philippians 1:6, *CEV*).

You just keep taking one more stop on the life path that He has set out for you . . . and He will do the work on the inside of you. He has promised that He will meet your every need: "This same God who takes care of me will supply all your needs from his glorious riches, which have been given to us in Christ Jesus" (Philippians 4:19, *NLT*).

Other people might break their promises, but God never will. Let's do more than believe *in* God; let's believe God.

Daily Step

What areas are you being impatient about right now? Ask God to forgive you . . . and then say Philippians 1:6 out loud.

Day 16

*For I know the thoughts and plans that I have for you, says
the Lord, thoughts and plans for welfare and peace and not
for evil, to give you hope in your final outcome.*

JEREMIAH 29:11, *AMP*

---

wel·fare *n:* health, happiness, and good fortune; well-being

peace *n:* inner contentment; serenity

hope *v:* to look forward to with confidence or expectation

Some people are afraid of God. They think He is mad at them. Some
people picture God as this far-off angry being. Perhaps they even
picture Him randomly looking for people who blow it so that He
can crush them. God gets blamed for quite a bit. But I want to tell
you . . . the God we serve is *good*. He loves us . . . uncondition-
ally . . . regardless of whether we will ever love Him or not.

God is not mad at you.

It doesn't matter where you have come from or what you have
done . . . God's plans for you have not and will not change.

I was recently talking to a young girl who looked at me with
so much pain in her eyes. She had been abused and hurt for so

many years that now she was living a lifestyle she was ashamed of . . . so much darkness and sin. In her eyes, she was beyond redemption. Imagine what happened when she began to hear that although she might have given up on God, He had never given up on her. Imagine what happened when she began to hear that God not only loved her but had a future filled with hope planned for her.

I'll tell you what happened . . . a changed life.

It did not happen overnight, but gradually, after hearing over and over and over again that hope could be hers, she began to believe it. And when she believed it, transformation occurred.

I have seen that same story happen many times. Lives are changed when hope is restored.

I love the words that Jeremiah penned. Look at them . . . these are God's plans and thoughts toward you: health, happiness, good fortune, well-being, inner contentment, serenity, to be able to confidently look forward with expectation. Wow! Never believe anything less.

Daily Step

Be honest with yourself . . . do you really believe that God's plans for you are health, happiness, good fortune, well-being, inner contentment and serenity? The Bible says they are. Are you willing to believe it?

Day 17

*Therefore if any person is [ingrafted] in Christ (the Messiah)
he is a new creation (a new creature altogether); the old
[previous moral and spiritual condition] has passed away.
Behold, the fresh and new has come!*

2 CORINTHIANS 5:17, *AMP*

Just today I said something to my husband that I shouldn't have. And yesterday I was pretty inconsiderate of a friend. And the day before that, I found myself still carrying a grudge (OK . . . it was a little one!) against someone.

Last week I said something about someone to someone else that I shouldn't have . . . I'm pretty sure that God would call it gossiping. And there was a time in college when I cheated on a test. And there was a season, as a young woman, that I turned my back on God.

We have all made mistakes. Maybe yours look like mine, or maybe yours are not so bad, or perhaps they are even worse. Doesn't matter. We have all missed it.

Sometimes we are our own worst enemy. If we are not careful, we can find ourselves carrying around a ton of guilt and then wondering why we are not free.

And just as bad, sometimes we try to heap guilt on others. Maybe someone you know has had a horrible and sad past . . .

drugs . . . promiscuity . . . suicide attempts . . . abortions . . . the list can go on.

But the Word of God says that if anyone is in Christ . . . she is a new creation. I love that. If *anyone*. Anyone. Regardless of what kind of life you lived, regardless of what you did last week, if you put your faith in Him . . . you are a new person. I am a new person.

What tripped me up last week does not have to be what messes me up this week. Your faith in Jesus makes you a new creation . . . clean, whole, pure. Don't let the enemy or anyone else tell you that you are not good enough. Without Jesus, none of us are good enough. With Him, we are brand new. With Him, we can live the life that we were designed to live.

Daily Step

Thank God that you are not who you used to be. Describe the new creation that you are now . . . write it down (maybe use words like forgiven, healed, free from_____, full of love, patient, and so forth).

Day 18

She is clothed with strength and dignity, and she laughs with no fear of the future. When she speaks, her words are wise, and kindness is the rule when she gives instructions.

PROVERBS 31:25-26, NLT

I often wonder how much of our time is spent thinking about all the things we should do, or worse, *should be.*

"I should work out more. I should eat better. I should budget my money. I should try harder to work out this relationship with my dad . . . brother . . . mom . . . friend . . . coworker. I should spend more time with my friends. I should be a *better* friend. I should be more passionate . . . honest . . . loving . . . encouraging . . . understanding."

The list could go on for days, *if* we were honest with ourselves. I think this is one of the enemy's greatest tactics in our lives. He keeps us focused on all the things we *should be* instead of all the things *we are.* Whereas God describes us as we really are . . . clothed in strength and dignity . . . laughing with no fear of the future. He says your words are wise . . . *wow!* . . . and that kindness rules your life.

So there you go. You may not have bulging biceps (me neither!), but you are clothed by your Creator with strength and dignity both in character and in heart. And you can laugh with no fear of tomorrow!

So no more worries about what you *should* do—you are released to giggle with your girlfriends or your children without holding back, which means you are free in your Maker to just *be*. By knowing God, you can also know wisdom.

Proverbs 2:12 tells us that wisdom will save us: "Wisdom will save you from evil people, from those whose speech is corrupt" (*NLT*). Proverbs 3:13-14 states that wisdom is more profitable than silver and gold: "God blesses everyone who has wisdom and common sense. Wisdom is worth more than silver; it makes you much richer than gold" (*CEV*).

Wisdom sees people where they are and is kind enough to always speak to the treasure inside of their heart, hence allowing them to *be*. There is a treasure in your soul that your heavenly Father is always speaking to.

So, my friend . . . pursue the voice of wisdom and you will find all that you are . . . and all that you need.

Daily Step

Read Proverbs 2 and 3. Write down any verses that will help you grow in wisdom today.

Day 19

*GOD, investigate my life; get all the facts firsthand.
I'm an open book to you; even from a distance, you know
what I'm thinking. You know when I leave and when I get
back; I'm never out of your sight. You know everything
I'm going to say before I start the first sentence. I look behind
me and you're there, then up ahead and you're there, too—
your reassuring presence, coming and going. This is
too much, too wonderful—I can't take it all in!*

PSALM 139:1-6, *THE MESSAGE*

I remember playing hide and seek with my children when they were really little. When it was their turn to "hide," I used to laugh. They would simply cover their eyes and think that because they couldn't see me, I couldn't see them. They seemed so surprised when I "found" them!

Perhaps there have been times in your life when you wish God wasn't watching. Maybe you have tried to hide from Him by closing your eyes . . . and to Him you probably looked just like my kids looked to me!

But I would imagine that most of us are very glad that we are never out of God's sight. I have been on a scary journey this year, and yet I can be at peace because God knows all about my journey.

He is behind me and up ahead of me. Wherever I go, there He is. I am never alone. He was with me when I heard the diagnosis of cancer. He was with me in the midst of some tough treatments.

God knows all the stages of my life. He knows all of yours, too. He will be with you on that job interview. He will be with you when you say "I do" to the man you marry. He will be with you when the marriage goes through a tough time.

He will be with you when you give birth. He will be with you when your children graduate from high school . . . He will be with you when your nest is empty . . . He will be with you when you hold your first grandchild. He will be with you when you breathe your last breath. He will be with you as you step into eternity. You are never out of His sight.

As the psalmist said, "It is too wonderful."

Daily Step

Describe the stage of life you are in. Thank God for being with you in the middle of this stage.

Day 20

Be content with who you are, and don't put on airs. God's strong hand is on you, he'll promote you at the right time. It won't be long before this generous God who has great plans for us in Christ—eternal and glorious plans they are!— will have you put together and on your feet for good. He gets the last word; yes, he does.

1 PETER 5:6,11, *THE MESSAGE*

For a number of years, I worked as an actress in Hollywood. I met some great people, and most of the time I really enjoyed the work. Really, who wouldn't like someone doing your hair and makeup every day??

I also liked the craft of acting. It was fun to become someone else, if only for a short while. On one particular assignment, I was playing a young girl who was not very nice. To stay in character, even between takes, I would have an arrogant expression on my face. On another job I was playing a young woman with an eating disorder, so even between takes I had a slightly haunted expression going on. Another time, I was playing a young girl with a mischievous edge. So yes, I had quite a bit of fun being the troublemaker on the set that day!

But while it might be entertaining to be someone else for a moment, trying to live that way is a waste of time. Work hard at being content with who you are. God's hand is on the real you . . . not the you that you wish you were. Yes, we should all be growing and making changes to overcome weaknesses . . . but we should not waste one moment trying to be someone else.

Imagine a baseball team. The pitcher is not wasting a moment whining that he is not the catcher. The girl on first base is not complaining that she is not the pitcher. Rather, all these players are working hard to be the best at the positions they have been assigned.

Remember, when God created you, He threw out the mold. You are unique . . . one of a kind. Trust that your Father has His hand on you. He will promote you at the right time. He does get the last word!

Daily Step

Think about whether you have been trying to be someone else. Have you been playing a role? Are you wearing a mask?

Day 21

*For we do not have a great high priest who is unable
to sympathize with our weaknesses, but we have one who
has been tempted in every way, just as we are—yet was
without sin. Let us then approach the throne of grace with
confidence, so that we may receive mercy and find
grace to help us in our time of need.*

HEBREWS 4:15-16, *NIV*

I was very blessed as a child. I had (and have!) an earthly father who loves me. I was told every day that I was loved. His arms were always open to me.

When I was hurt or afraid, my father would engulf me in his embrace. I could just run right to him and most of my needs would get met. Even as a young girl, I knew that my dad's lap was one of the safest places to be. I could confidently approach him.

If you did not have a father who lovingly embraced you . . . you do now. Right now you can confidently approach your heavenly Father. His arms are open wide. All of the mercy and grace that you need is found in His arms.

He is ready . . . always . . . to help. He is never too busy. He has all the time you need.

Perhaps it will take courage to approach Him because you have never been loved by a father before . . . and maybe you think your heavenly Father is like the one you knew. Maybe you think that you will be criticized, judged and then abandoned.

Nope. Not by your Father in heaven.

He loves you . . . just the way you are. He loves you and is very aware of your imperfections. He loves you eternally and without fail. There is nothing that you have done or will do that can separate you from the love of God.

So go ahead, confidently approach your God. Let His arms and His love surround you.

Daily Step

Make a decision today that when you approach God, it will be with confidence . . . confidence that His arms are open to you . . . confidence that He wants to hear from you . . . and confidence that you are loved.

Day 22

But God put his love on the line for us by offering his Son in sacrificial death while we were of no use whatever to him.

ROMANS 5:8, *THE MESSAGE*

God did not keep back his own Son, but he gave him for us. If God did this, won't he freely give us everything else?

ROMANS 8:32, *CEV*

I remember the first kiss that Philip and I shared . . . a little timidity, a little passion and a lot of heart . . . all mixed together as our lips touched. (And actually, I remember wondering if my breath was OK!)

I love the end of a fairy tale when the hero and the heroine kiss. There is something that happens when two people share true love's kiss.

At the end of the movie *Shrek,* we saw the hero, Shrek, kiss Fiona. There was a lot of light, stars, fairy dust and romantic music . . . you know, a real Hollywood moment.

Fiona had the unfortunate tendency of turning into an ogre when night fell, and this kiss—true love's kiss, according to the story—was supposed to keep her in her beautiful human form. But when the stardust faded, she was still an ogre.

As Fiona looked at Shrek, she was a little sad, because she said the kiss was supposed to make her beautiful. Shrek looked tenderly in her eyes and said, "But you are beautiful."

God kissed humanity by sending Jesus. And because of Jesus, we are beautiful in our Father's eyes.

Sometimes because of what you have been through in life, you may not feel beautiful . . . but the kiss of heaven, the kiss of your heavenly Father, has made you beautiful.

His kiss tenderly touches you. His eyes gaze upon you with true love . . . a love that is beyond compare. His kiss declares your beauty. His kiss declares your value. His kiss declares that you are forgiven.

Lift up your face and let true love's kiss . . . the one that matters most, the kiss of heaven . . . touch it.

Daily Step

Close your eyes, and be thankful that you have received heaven's kiss.

Kiss me again and again, for your love is sweeter than wine.

SONG OF SOLOMON 1:2, *NLT*

Day 23

Kings' daughters are among Your honorable women.

PSALM 45:9, *AMP*

I love a good chick flick. Mainly because most of them end with a version of happily ever after! And actually I see nothing wrong with that. I thoroughly got into watching *Ever After* and *A Cinderella Story* with my daughter. I loved that at some point in the movie, both girls had crowns on their heads. Those were fairy tales . . . or at least modern versions of one. You, my friend, are a princess, and this has nothing to do with fairy tales. The *reality* is that you are a thriving, preciously fashioned, loved-beyond-measure daughter of the King.

The prophet Ezekiel painted an awesome picture of how loved and valued you are. Here is my version of what he said: God is not afraid of the messes that surround you. Maybe you feel unloved. You could have been abandoned, mistreated, abused. Maybe you still are. Perhaps no one in your world has extended a hand of compassion toward you. Doesn't matter . . . God always comes to the rescue. He steps into the middle of your mess, grabs your hand, causes you to grow, to flourish . . . to change. He has even made an unbreakable covenant with you by calling you His own. He washes your wounds, cleans up your past, and anoints you for your future. He has dressed you in the finest royal garments and adorned you with rare jewels. To finish His glorious creation, He places a crown on your beautiful head.

A crown.

Not rags, but royal clothing and a crown. When your Father sees you, He sees you with a crown on your head. You are royalty. You are a princess. Being His daughter *makes* you a princess . . . regardless of what you feel like . . . regardless of your past.

There is something wonderful that happens in our little girl heart when we truly realize the truth. Our princess life is not a fairy tale; it is a fact. We are the loved-beyond-measure daughter of a King.

Daily Step

OK . . . this might seem weird, but do it anyway. Find a crown, any crown . . . Burger King, plastic costume or full on rhinestone . . . and put it on your head. Just for a few moments, get a look at how God truly sees you (don't forget to take it off before you go to work!).

Day 24

*My choice is you, GOD, first and only. And now I find
I'm your choice! You set me up with a house and a yard.
And then you make me your heir!*

PSALM 16:5-6, *THE MESSAGE*

Do you remember the agony of physical education in elementary school?

The games weren't so bad; it was the team selection process that was painful for most people. I am a fairly athletic person, so I was always one of the first chosen on most teams (at least, one of the first girls!). There was such a sense of value and relief (!) when I heard my name called.

However, I remember feeling very sad for a few people who were always chosen last. And in fact, I remember the captains saying things like, "It's your turn [talking to the other captain] to have so and so; they are so awful."

Yes, it was bad enough for those kids to be chosen last, but it was utterly humiliating to have other kids talking about how pathetic they were. (Of course, those children who were chosen last are probably now CEOs of major companies!)

The good news is that God chose you first! He did not sigh and then say, "OK, I guess I have to have you." No way. When He was selecting His teams, He looked right at you and wanted you on His side. He created you with your gifts, abilities and talents, knowing that His team would be lacking if you weren't on it.

And then, beyond making you a team member, He made you His heir . . . and gave you your share of the inheritance.

in·her·it *v:* to receive (property or a title, for example) from an ancestor by legal succession or will

Part of God's inheritance for you is a new title. He calls you "princess." He chose you first, and then He set you up to be successful as His heir.

From all that He has, He has given you a love that is beyond compare, acceptance, dignity, prosperity, health, value . . . and heaven! This is your inheritance.

As His daughter . . . His princess . . . you have the right to all that He has. Will you take it?

Daily Step

What do you think you bring to God's team?

Day 25

Now listen, daughter, don't miss a word: forget your country, put your home behind you. Be here—the king is wild for you. Since he's your lord, adore him. Set your mind now on sons.

PSALM 45:10-11,16, *THE MESSAGE*

"You don't understand, Holly; some horrible things were done to me. There is no way I am a princess. My father abused me for five years as a child; my mom just pretended nothing was going on. No one really cared about me or even really saw me. For so many years I hated being female, and then as a young woman I became a stripper. I used my body to entice men . . . hating them all the while."

I have heard this story (or one like it) many times. Truly, it breaks my heart. A young girl, created as a daughter of the King, gets hurt and abused by those who should be extending the love of God to her.

Yes, many of us have stories similar to this one. It still doesn't change who we are. There is nothing you have done that disqualifies you from being God's daughter.

Your challenge is to put your past behind you. That is the challenge the psalmist sets forth in this Scripture. Forget where you came from; put your home and your past . . . hurts and all . . . behind you.

Perhaps you had some horrible years. I am not saying to pretend that they did not happen; I am saying, don't let yesterday's pain keep you from the beautiful future that God has designed for you.

Too many times, we let the past limit our future . . . even if our past was a good one. Perhaps you had some awesome times in your yesterdays . . . you got straight *As*, won a beauty pageant, gave a great speech, got a scholarship, shot the game-winning basket, whatever. If you are not careful, those will become the "good old days" for you, and you won't be able to focus on where God wants to take you.

Be here—in the present. Your King is wild for you!

And then, begin to focus on tomorrow . . . that is what is meant by "set your mind now on sons." Instead of being guilty, anxious or weighed down by who you used to be, focus on who you are and are becoming.

We actually have an obligation as daughters of the King to move beyond our past and to smile at our future (see Proverbs 31:25).

Daily Step

Read Philippians 3:13-14. How can you apply this verse to your life today?

Why do you now cry aloud—have you no king?
. . . Now many nations are gathered against you.
But they do not know the thoughts of the Lord;
they do not understand his plan, he who gathers
them like sheaves to the threshing floor.

MICAH 4:9,11-12, *NIV*

I was sitting on my bed, trying not to freak out over the fact that I had been diagnosed with cancer.

There have been other moments when I have been at my wits end (wherever that is!?) about how to handle my teenage son.

There were days that I felt hopeless in the midst of another marriage crisis.

I have cried over the injustice I see on display around the world.

And, like you, my heart has been broken over the betrayal of friends.

There are moments when we have all felt as if our life was spinning out of control. I am sure you have had those times when you were confused and didn't know what to do.

Maybe your family was going through a crisis . . . and you couldn't see the light at the end of the tunnel. Maybe you were scared about whether or not you could really do the job you were hired to do. Maybe you were not sure what to do about your aging parents.

Life is full of challenges . . . Jesus told us that.

But the great news is . . . we have a King! I love this verse in Micah. I have heard it in my heart a number of times.

"Hey, Holly . . . why are you crying? Why are you freaking out? Don't you serve the most high King?"

Right.

I am not alone . . . the most powerful King of all is not even a breath away.

So that means I can come to Him as a daughter and trust that He will help me navigate the tough moments.

He will help you, too. He will send His Holy Spirit to bring comfort. If you ask, He will give you the wisdom you need to not only get you through whatever you are dealing with at the moment but also to help someone else get through it as well.

Dry your tears, daughter . . . there is a King that lives among you.

Daily Step

Take a breath, lift your face toward heaven and call out to your King.

Day 27

I love you, GOD—you make me strong. GOD is bedrock under my feet, the castle in which I live, my rescuing knight. My GOD—the high crag where I run for dear life, hiding behind the boulders, safe in the granite hideout. I sing to GOD, the Praise-Lofty, and find myself safe and saved.

PSALM 18:1-3, *THE MESSAGE*

As a child, I knew that I was loved and could just run into the presence of my dad. I knew that whatever I needed would be taken care of. I knew I was loved and that he delighted in me. I didn't have to do anything to earn his love.

However, as that young girl, rarely, if ever, did I ask my dad what I could do for him. I was just focused on what I wanted from him. That's okay as a child, but as an adult, occasionally I ask my dad if there is anything I can do for him. Does he need a cup of coffee? A glass of water? A hug? or whatever.

I have a daughter, Paris, and she is very sure of the love of her daddy. She freely comes to him with many of her needs . . . stuff for her horse . . . basketball information . . . affection . . . money . . . a chat . . . a hug . . . and lots of love!

Right now, she is on that bridge between a woman and a child, and *occasionally* she thinks of what her dad would like. I pray that eventually she will think more and more of others . . . not just her needs.

I think it is the same with God. We all come to Him as daughters, but at some point we need to make the transition from child to woman.

My friend Bobbie Houston said it like this: "We become a lover of God when we seek to discover the throne room." A woman comes into the throne room confident of her position. She comes in, confident that the Father always meets her needs, and yet she comes in not to get but to give.

She comes in to love the Father. She seeks His heart, not just His hand, and she asks, "What can I get You? What can I do for You, Father? What can I do to help build Your kingdom?"

Yes, we are princesses . . . but let's be grown-up ones.

Daily Step

How do you see yourself approaching God? Are you the child princess or the woman princess . . . or maybe a little of both?

Day 28

Arise, shine, for your light has come, and the glory of the LORD rises upon you. See, darkness covers the earth and thick darkness is over the peoples, but the LORD rises upon you and his glory appears over you. Nations will come to your light, and kings to the brightness of your dawn.

ISAIAH 60:1-3, *NIV*

I gotta tell you, I can sooooooo do the princess thing! I get a great kick out of this thought when I am with my friends getting a pedicure, a new hairstyle, or incredible service at an upscale restaurant.

I have been to amazing spas where it seemed like every part of my body was worked on . . . all at once . . . and I loved it! Seriously . . . who doesn't?

To be honest, I don't see one reason why I shouldn't love the luxuries in life. After all, I am a daughter of the King! And so are you! But we can never confuse the reason that God has made us a princess during this time in history. We are not princesses to be served, but to serve.

The original establishment of royal families all over the earth was for the purpose of serving humanity. Those who are royalty are partly a guardian force over the people they rule. Regardless of how the current royals may or may not have strayed from their purpose, we cannot stray from our own.

Since you and I are princesses in the greatest royal family of all, we must understand our responsibility to serve humanity. This understanding comes from realizing our role and recognizing that we have access to all that the Father has in order to freely give what has already been given to you.[2]

So, princess . . . arise and shine, for your light has come . . . the glory of your King is upon you. Why? Because darkness covers the earth and it's people.

Your King has put His light on you so that others would see . . . see His glory, see His love—just see Him . . . and then you could lead the lost and hurting to Him.

Yes, you are a princess. It's all about you . . . and not about you at all.

Daily Step

Who in your world needs to really understand that she is the priceless daughter of a King? Go tell her.

The bride, the beautiful princess, a royal daughter, is glorious.
She waits within her chamber, dressed in a gown woven with
gold. Wearing the finest garments, she is brought to the King.
Her friends, her companions, follow her into the royal palace.
What a joyful, enthusiastic, excited procession as they enter
the palace! She comes before her King, who is wild for her!

PSALM 45:13-15, AUTHOR'S ADAPTATION

A few years ago, I was teaching at a conference and a young woman approached me. She told me that when I had been at this particular conference the year before, I had taught about being the princess chick. She reminded me that I had placed plastic crowns on a few of the women in the audience to illustrate the point. She said that when I did that, a light bulb went on for her . . . and she got it. She needed to understand her royal position and all that comes with it so that she could be an illustration for others.

A few months later, she went on a mission trip to East Africa. She put a few crowns in her suitcase (never leave home without at least one!!). She had the opportunity to minister to some young women . . . and showed me a photo. The photo brought tears to my eyes. Here was a group of young African women, sitting in a mud hut, with crowns on their heads. She was teaching them all about their value.

How cool is that??

You and I have an obligation to live our lives as princesses. And it is not just for us. It is so that our *friends and our companions will follow us into the royal palace.*

When you understand that you are the loved-beyond-measure daughter of the King, you will live your life differently. You will know your worth and not let anyone treat you less than a royal daughter. You will not abuse others or your own body . . . because royal princesses don't behave that way. When you understand that you are designed to serve humanity as God's princess, then you can freely give . . . and you have an obligation to do so.

And when you know this, you will affect the women who are in your world . . . who will effect the women in theirs . . . until eventually it will go around the globe.

Imagine a planet in which every woman understands her worth and knows that she is the loved, irreplaceable daughter of the King. Wow.

Daily Step

*What would your world look like
if the women in it understood
about being His princesses?*

Day 30

I waited patiently for the LORD to help me, and he turned to me and heard my cry. He lifted me out of the pit of despair, out of the mud and the mire. He set my feet on solid ground and steadied me as I walked along. He has given me a new song to sing, a hymn of praise to our God. Many will see what he has done and be astounded. They will put their trust in the LORD.

PSALM 40:1-3, *NLT*

I was watching some television show where the hero got caught in a quicksand or mud pit that was slowly pulling him down. The more he thrashed around, the quicker he sank. Finally, he became still and called out for help. His friend heard him, came and, with the help of a rope, slowly pulled him out of the slimy pit.

I have stepped in the occasional mud puddle, but I have never been fully immersed in a literal pit of mud and mire. That sounds very gross. I have, however, been immersed in the pit of despair. A few times actually. One time was when my marriage was at its darkest moment. Another time was when my doctor said that the lump was cancer.

I did know enough to realize that I needed to call out to God during these moments. And when I did, He lifted me up and out of my pit of despair. I realized that my being lifted out and set on solid ground was not just for me . . . but also so that other princesses around me could have hope that they could be lifted out too.

There have been quite a few women who have been encouraged to continue working at their own marriages because they saw me move from despair to solid ground. And there have been women who have been astounded at how I am navigating the cancer journey. My faith in my God has caused them to put their trust in Him.

And that's what it's all about.

Whatever pit you might be in . . . your God will get you out because He loves you . . . and because He loves the women who are watching to see how you handle it.

In the book of Acts, we read the story of Paul and Silas being thrown into prison. And while in prison, they sang praises to God. I guess they could have complained that the treatment wasn't fair, that they were wrongly imprisoned, or something like that. But no—in the midst of the disgusting prison cell, they worshiped their God. And one verse tells us that the other prisoners were listening. I would imagine that these prisoners were encouraged too.

You know what, princess? There are prisoners in your world . . . and they are watching you.

Daily Step

Do you feel a sense of obligation to live your life as a daughter of the King? Who in your world is watching you?

Day 31

Put on your sword, powerful warrior . . . Win the victory for what is true and right. Your power will do amazing things.

PSALM 45:3-4, NCV

In your majesty, ride out to victory, defending truth, humility, and justice. Go forth to perform awe-inspiring deeds!

PSALM 45:4, NLT

I was not a big fan of the thirty-first chapter of Proverbs . . . mainly because the woman was described as "virtuous." And to me, that just sounded weak and wimpy. It is sort of like describing Jesus as meek and lowly, when He is actually a fierce warrior . . . like Mel Gibson in *Braveheart* or Viggo Mortensen in *Lord of the Rings* . . . only better.

Well, I discovered that "virtuous" actually means "a force on the earth."[3] How about that? The "virtuous woman" of Proverbs 31 is like her Creator—a fierce warrior! She is a woman deeply connected to people, a woman with the means to help provide an incredible life, and a woman with a well of resources to draw from in time of need. Not only do you have a crown on your head . . . you have a sword in your hand!

The psalmist tells us that we are to win the victory for what is true and right. We are warriors on the earth sent to defend truth and justice.

What does it mean to be a warrior? How can I become this warrior? What are the qualities of a good soldier?

A warrior has courage.

cour·age *n:* the state or quality of mind or spirit that enables one to face danger, fear, with self-possession, confidence, and resolution; bravery

America is called "the home of the brave." If there's ever been a time when we needed people to be brave, it's now. Thousands of Americans have risked their lives to help hurting people in devastated parts of our country and around the world. Unwilling to turn a blind eye, they left comfort, rolled up their sleeves, and did what they could do . . . brave. Maybe you have forgiven someone when what you wanted to do was smack them . . . brave. Maybe you had an uncomfortable conversation with someone when you would much rather have just withdrawn . . . brave. Maybe you risked your heart again . . . brave.

You are a warrior. You were designed to be brave.

Daily Step

What is something that you are afraid to do? Is it time to be brave and do it?

Day 32

*She rises while it is yet night and gets [spiritual] food for
her household and assigns her maids their tasks.*

PROVERBS 31:15, *AMP*

I learned an interesting lesson at my daughter's science fair.
Turns out, back in the '90s, a few scientists got together and created a synthetic environment called "Biosphere 2." They lived
inside it for two years . . . without a Starbucks and without a
shoe store (who had that bright idea? ☺). They generated almost
every state of weather, except wind, in this self-contained atmo-
sphere. Because of the lack of wind, it did not take long before
the trees began to bow, contort, and even snap.

I realized that we are not too different from the trees (minus
the bark on our skin). If there is no pressure from the wind, the
trunks of trees grow too weak to even hold up their own weight.
In the same way, if there is no weathering the wind of storms in
our own lives, there will not be enough strength to hold us as we
are growing. Maneuvering and enduring the winds of change
and adversity builds strength in our character and our heart.

I like sleeping "while it is yet night," so I wasn't too crazy
about this verse. Well, I have some good news! After I did some
studying, I found out that this verse has more meaning then just
the time of day you wake up. I was happy to hear that . . .

although what it does mean is certainly challenging enough!

This verse is talking about you . . . the warrior . . . rising in the midst of adversity, in the midst of chaos, in the midst of trouble, in the midst of dark times. You, this awesome force on the earth, are designed to be the one who rises with courage when others are freaking out. (Maybe getting up early now sounds easier. ☺)

By letting fear overtake you, it will not only limit you but also could very well hurt others. We need to take the focus off ourselves and be the warriors for a family, a city and a world that so desperately need to see courage in action. There are times when we all feel afraid. Courage is doing the right thing in spite of the fear.

The eyes of our Father are looking all over the earth for this warrior princess—a woman who is willing and brave enough to rise in the dark . . . make the hard decision . . . risk her time for someone else . . . share her story so that someone else can be free. C'mon, raise your hand . . . you are the woman He is looking for!

Daily Step

Think of one person you know who has risen above in the midst of a hard time. What qualities does she possess that give her the courage to rise above? Are those qualities at work in you? Which ones do you need to strengthen?

Day 33

As for me, my life has already been poured out
as an offering to God. The time of my death is near.
I have fought a good fight, I have finished the race,
and I have remained faithful.

2 TIMOTHY 4:6-7, *NLT*

One of the first women to make the journey across the Rocky Mountains was Narcissa Whitman. The year was 1836 and she was traveling with her husband and one other couple. Her life, as well as the lives of all pioneer women, was difficult.

Narcissa and Marcus worked together in order to bring the gospel of Jesus Christ to the natives, the Cayuse people. A little over 10 years later, many of the natives died from an epidemic of measles. They began to accuse the Whitmans of using evil to kill their people, and fear began to rise up among them.

A few of the Cayuse people barged into the Whitman home and murdered both Marcus and Narcissa. It is noted that some of her last words were, "Tell my sister that I died at my post."

Warriors stay at their posts.

I don't think God necessarily requires that we die at our post, but I do think He requires us to stay at our post. I don't know to which posts you have been assigned, but I know mine. I have the post of wife, so even when Philip makes me angry or hurts my feelings, I can't just run off with the first cute man that comes along.

I have been assigned the post of mother, so even when my children are at their brattiest, I can't abandon them or ship them off to Siberia (although I have been tempted!).

I also stand at the post of pastor, so I must remain faithful, even when I am disappointed by people.

I have the post of friend, so I spend time keeping in touch with all of the wonderful people around the world that God has sent across my path.

I also have the post of teacher, so even if I want to play all day, I don't because I have messages to prepare.

All good and faithful warriors stay at the post to which they have been assigned.

Daily Step

How about you? Can you remain faithful at the posts that God has entrusted you with?

Day 34

God is strong, and he wants you strong. So take everything the Master has set out for you, well-made weapons of the best materials. And put them to use so you will be able to stand up to everything the Devil throws your way. This is no afternoon athletic contest that we'll walk away from and forget about in a couple of hours.

EPHESIANS 6:10-12, *THE MESSAGE*

strong *adj:* capable of withstanding force or wear; solid, tough, or firm

This isn't a game we are playing or an "afternoon athletic contest" that we will "forget about in a couple of hours." God has awesome plans for us. Perfect plans. But they aren't just handed to us on a silver platter. Many times we have to fight for them.

We have an enemy, Satan, and the last thing he wants is for you and me to be walking in God's plans and God's will. He will do whatever it takes to knock us off course. He will tempt us, throw sickness our way, and toss out challenges and troubles . . . all to see if we can be taken off course.

You and I have to determine that any plan that the enemy has will fail. He will not take us out. We will live every day fulfilling God's will for us. We must make a decision to believe that no weapon formed against us will prosper. "No weapon forged against you will prevail, and you will refute every tongue that accuses you" (Isaiah 54:17, *NIV*). Weapons will be formed against us—no doubt about that!—but they will not prosper.

God wants you to be strong in Him. Being strong is what will enable you to "still be on your feet" at the end of the battle. Determine that you will be the warrior who can withstand whatever comes your way.

Raise your sword, warrior princess, and remember for whom you are fighting.

Daily Step

What area in your life could you be stronger in?

Be prepared. You're up against far more than you can handle on your own. Take all the help you can get, every weapon God has issued, so that when it's all over but the shouting you'll still be on your feet.

EPHESIANS 6:12-13, *THE MESSAGE*

Day 35

I command you—be strong and courageous!
Do not be afraid or discouraged. For the LORD your
God is with you wherever you go.

JOSHUA 1:9, *NLT*

There was a time when women were not allowed to act on stage in the theatres. I know, I know . . . thank God we weren't born then! In the movie *Shakespeare in Love*, the main female character dresses as a man and goes by the name of Thomas Kent. She risks everything and auditions for the part of Romeo in *Romeo and Juliet*. She gets the part but is found out, and the theatre is closed down. So, the whole cast is ready to throw in the towel or drink themselves silly at the local pub, when a former enemy walks in and offers them a new stage on which to perform. The cast decides to take it.

Opening day comes, and they are in a mess. The narrator stutters, Juliet's voice breaks (all the actors are men, remember?), and Shakespeare has to play Romeo—and he is also in love with the ex-Romeo, who just that morning has been forced to marry someone she doesn't love . . . things look a little like disaster. The cast is also missing some essential pieces to their puzzle . . . like Juliet.

Lucky for them, the former Thomas Kent is in the audience, and she just happens to know every word. So, they call her to the stage. The backstage talk goes a little like this: "We'll all be put in the clink!" "See you in jail."

However, once again, this young woman is willing to risk it all . . . humiliation, rejection . . . all for love and for a cause bigger than herself. She abandons the status quo, fulfills her role, and gives an overwhelming performance beside the man she truly loves. In a time of having no right to make decisions, she makes an excellent one . . . and it does not go unnoticed.

Just as the Queen's soldiers march in with "thus saith the queen" and "in the name of her majesty" to stop the performance, the Queen, who has been sitting in the audience the entire time, removes her cloak and stands defiantly, stating, "Have a care with my name; you will wear it out." She does not rebuke Thomas Kent, but expresses her agreement with a performance showing true love onstage. She also communicates understanding at the strength it took to be a woman in a man's world.

strength *n:* the power to resist strain or stress; durability

A warrior is strong. But being strong means more than bench pressing 200 pounds (although that is impressive!) or being able to break a brick. It also means being willing to endure. It is doing the right thing over and over again, no matter how hard or how boring it gets. Besides, you never know who might be watching.

Daily Step

Read 2 Timothy 2:3. What does this verse say to you?

Day 36

Is not this the God who armed me, then aimed me in the right direction? You armed me well for this fight.

PSALM 18:32,38, *THE MESSAGE*

Every morning, I stand in my closet and look at the clothes from which I have to choose. I select my outfit for the day based on what I have to do. (And, to be honest . . . whether or not it needs ironing is a big factor!)

If I am going to the gym first, I put on workout gear; if I am going to the office, I put on office-wearing clothes; if I am sitting at my computer, I put on the baggy comfy stuff.

However, not once have the clothes just jumped out of the closet and put themselves on me. Nope. I have to dress myself.

It is the same with the armor that we have been given. We have to put it on. Intentionally. We have been given the best armor in order to fight the battles we will need to fight. We just have to put it on.

We have been given armor and weapons. We have been equipped both defensively and offensively. We are not just to do our best to keep from getting whipped by the enemy . . . no, we are to offensively take ground. We are to be more than conquerors. The apostle Paul put it this way:

Yet in all these things we are more than conquerors through Him who loved us. For I am persuaded that neither death nor life, nor angels nor principalities nor powers, nor things present nor things to come, nor height nor depth, nor any other created thing, shall be able to separate us from the love of God which is in Christ Jesus our Lord (Romans 8:37-39, *NKJV*).

We would never think of sending the soldiers currently representing our country off to war in shorts and a T-shirt. No way. We want them protected from attack and we want them to do damage to the enemy. They have been armed well.

So have you and I. God has armed us well for the battles that we are to wage. He has armed us and set us on the path of victory. Never forget that.

Daily Step

Read Romans 8:31-39. What do these verses say to you? What do they tell you about the love of Christ? Do you believe in your heart that nothing will seperate you from God's love?

Day 37

Stand firm then, with the belt of truth buckled around your waist, with the breastplate of righteousness in place.

EPHESIANS 6:14, *NIV*

I must confess that I liked the movie *GI Jane*. She was one tough chick! The language was pretty foul, so I don't recommend it, but I did like the part where she was putting her gun together. She practiced and practiced until she got it right. She knew what to do with her weapon. And in the movie *Gladiator*, Russell Crowe certainly knew how to put his armor on. He wasn't holding his shield, asking what it was. He knew what it was and how to use it.

How about you? Do you know the armor that God has given to you? Do you know how to use it?

I don't really wear a belt to hold my pants up, although I am aware some people do. I have a few belts, but they really serve no purpose other than to make a fashion statement. However, for the Roman soldier, the belt was a very important part of the uniform. It held the weapons that the soldier would need. He would put the belt on first and tie it firmly in place. It was tied so tightly that no matter how tough the battle was or how much the soldier moved, it stayed in place. The belt had to be in the right place in order for the soldier to have easy access to his weapons.

For us, the belt of truth should be the first thing we put on. Truth holds things in place for us. Our ability to use our weapons, and even our protection, comes from having God's truth as our belt. His truth must be our foundation if we are going to wage war against the enemy.

Another piece of armor is the breastplate. (I don't think I have one of these in my closet!) Paul tells us to put on our "breastplate of righteousness." The breastplate of the Roman soldier protected the tender part of his body, much like the bulletproof vest that our police officers wear. The breastplate protects organs, which includes our heart. If we are going to win any battle, our spiritual heart has to be protected. Our heart must be right with God.

When you walk in the righteousness of God, it is a weapon of defense against all lies, plans and accusations of our enemy, the devil. Being right with God means knowing who you are . . . the loved-beyond-measure daughter the King! Jesus put you in right standing with your Father. When you know that, you can defeat the lies of the enemy.

So, how about it, warrior chick . . . is your armor on?

Daily Step

Write down one truth from the Bible that you are going to use today. Keep that belt on!

Day 38

*And with your feet fitted with the readiness
that comes from the gospel of peace.*

EPHESIANS 6:15, *NIV*

I have another confession to make. I love shoes. Really.

When I am shopping, I will often buy the shoes first and then try to find an outfit to go with them. Sometimes shoe shopping can brighten my whole day. Pathetic, isn't it. Do I still have your respect?? Or maybe you are a little like me . . . just a little.

Well, just so we can feel good about our shoe craze . . . shoes *are* an important part of the weapons God gave us. (Of course, we already know that shoes can be weapons . . . ever been stepped on by a stiletto heel?)

I have heard that some historians think footwear was one of the greatest reasons why the Roman army was so victorious. (I love this! Shoes = victory!)

victory *n:* defeat of an enemy or opponent; success in a struggle against difficulties or an obstacle

The shoes that the Roman soldier wore looked more like vicious golf shoes than our modern day combat boots. Conical hobnails or spikes were placed on the soles of the soldiers' thick sandals, which provided him with leverage for a strong stance.

These shoes also provided the soldier with balance, which allowed for easier walking over rough ground. Those spikes definitely came in handy for walking all over the enemy. Yikes!

I learned in martial arts that the stance is one of the most important things to master. Being able to keep balance no matter what is thrown at you can be the difference between victory or defeat. A strong punch or an effective kick comes from a balanced and steady stance.

Our feet are to be fitted with peace. This peace will help you stand with your feet planted firmly on the Word of God and stay there . . . regardless of how intense the battle is. This peace will also protect you when you walk through the rough places and keep you steady in the heat of a battle.

Daily Step

Do you have your "peace" shoes on?
How will they help you to stand
with your feet firmly planted in
the Word of God?

Day 39

In addition to all this, take up the shield of faith, with which you can extinguish all the flaming arrows of the evil one.

EPHESIANS 6:16, *NIV*

Our family went to Sea World this past summer. We had an awesome time just being together. I actually consider it a small miracle when I can have the attention of both of my teenagers for a few days!! While we were at Sea World, we saw the Shamu show. Wow! It was a pretty spectacular sight to see those big whales moving in unison.

There are two locations that one can choose to sit in at the show: the dry zone or the soak zone. My daughter and I were feeling brave, so we decided to sit in the soak zone. What was I thinking?

At one particular point in the show, a few of the whales came close to the glass and "waved," which means that they used their fins to splash the audience. As a huge wave of water headed toward us, the lady in front of me opened her umbrella and used it like a shield, deflecting most of the water from us. She was definitely a quick thinker . . . and I was grateful!

Part of the armor that you and I are to wear on this journey through life is our shield of faith.

Roman soldiers used a large oblong shield that protected them from arrow attacks. It was made of wood and was covered with leather or metal. During times of combat, the enemy would launch a bunch of arrows toward the soldiers.

The arrows often were wrapped in cloth, soaked in pitch and then set on fire. These flaming arrows could inflict serious damage. However, the leather covering on the Roman soldier's shield was often soaked in water so that when the fiery arrow hit the shield, it was extinguished.

You and I have an enemy—Satan—and he continues to shoot his fiery arrows at us. I don't know what missiles he has fired your way . . . maybe fear, doubt, guilt, shame, sickness, discouragement or hopelessness. But I do know that the only way you can extinguish those arrows is with your shield of faith.

Where are you placing your faith? Do you believe that no matter how fierce the battle, your heavenly Father is watching over you? Is your faith in Him and His promises?

Daily Step

Read Hebrews 11:1 and Psalm 91:1-4.
Can you put your faith in the fact that
God's promises are your armor?

Day 40

*Take the helmet of salvation and the sword of the Spirit, which
is the word of God. And pray in the Spirit on all occasions
with all kinds of prayers and requests. With this in mind, be
alert and always keep on praying for all the saints.*

EPHESIANS 6:17-18, *NIV*

We have a rule in our house: You can't ride your horse without a
helmet.

Both my husband and my daughter, who are the big riders in
our family, wear helmets when they are out riding horses. Paris
has a prettier helmet that she wears during horse shows, but
both her practice helmet and her show helmet have the same
purpose—to protect her head.

Roman soldiers wore helmets made of iron to protect their
heads. These helmets protected the entire head . . . two hinged
sidepieces protected the soldiers' jaw and cheekbone; a long
piece of metal at the back of the helmet protected their necks.
The soldiers knew that one blow to the head could kill, so they
did not forget to put on their helmets before going into battle.

You and I are to put on the helmet of salvation. This helmet
is designed to guard our minds. In the midst of warfare, we must
have a strong mind. The mind is the source for every action we
take, every decision we make, and every thought that we allow to

linger. Every behavior we exhibit begins in our mind.

The helmet of salvation gives us confidence in Christ. You and I have been saved by what Christ did for us on the cross. God didn't establish a relationship with us because of our goodness. No . . . we can only come into the presence of God because of what Jesus did for us. No one can take that away.

Satan will attack our minds with discouragement. He loves to point out our weaknesses. He not only wants us to doubt our salvation but also God's goodness and whether our life has value. The helmet of salvation protects our minds from the attacks of the enemy. It assures us of how great a love God has for us.

Make sure yours is on.

Daily Step

*Don't worry about helmet hair!
Make sure the helmet of salvation is
securely fastened upon your head.*

*But let us who live in the light think clearly,
protected by the body armor of faith and love,
and wearing as our helmet the confidence
of our salvation.*

1 THESSALONIANS 5:8, *NLT*

Day 41

*For the Word that God speaks is alive and full of power
[making it active, operative, energizing, and effective]; it is
sharper than any two-edged sword, penetrating to the dividing line of the breath of life (soul) and [the immortal] spirit,
and of joints and marrow [of the deepest parts of our
nature], exposing and sifting and analyzing and judging
the very thoughts and purposes of the heart.*

HEBREWS 4:12, *AMP*

The offensive weapon that we have been given is the Word of
God. The sword that Roman soldiers used was about 18 inches
long and sharp on both sides. The Greek translation of "word"
in this verse is *rhema* in Hebrew. Rhema implies an utterance, a
spoken word. This verse tells us that the Word of God is sharper
than any two-edged sword. So let's use it!

When the devil was trying to mess with Jesus in the wilder-
ness, Jesus fought him by speaking the Word of God back to
him. Three times the devil tried to tempt Jesus, and three times
Jesus rebuked him with Scripture. After the devil's third
attempt, Jesus cried, "Away from me, Satan! *For it is written:
'Worship the Lord your God, and serve him only'*" (Matthew
4:10, *NIV*, emphasis added). It was the spoken Word that
brought victory.

In my battle this year, I have spent hours walking in my room, quoting the Word of God out loud. When the threats of the enemy sound off in my head, I just make my shouts louder! Speak His Word.

And do you know what? You have to practice to engage in this kind of battle. I have read many books about warriors from many different countries and different eras, and the one thing they all did was practice. They spent hours practicing with their swords. They practiced until their swords felt like an extension of their own arm.

> *Training remains strict to enforce the belief that the more you sweat in peacetime, the less you will bleed in war.*
> —quote from Navy SEAL

Become familiar with God's Word . . . so familiar that in the midst of your unseen battles you can readily speak it out loud. And pray . . . pray for yourself and for others in the midst of their battles.

Daily Step

Memorize three verses in the Bible that relate to a situation you are going through. (You can find some in the back of this devotional to get you started.)

By means of his one Spirit, we all said good-bye to our partial and piecemeal lives. We each used to independently call our own shots, but then we entered into a large and integrated life in which he has the final say in everything . . . each of us is now a part of his resurrection body, refreshed and sustained at one fountain—his Spirit—where we all come to drink. . . . What we have is one body with many parts, each its proper size and in its proper place. No part is important on its own.

1 CORINTHIANS 12:12-13,25, *THE MESSAGE*

There is one rule that all the elite fighting forces of the world have . . . soldiers are never deployed alone. True warriors know that they are part of a team. They know that they will not win the battle on their own. Navy SEALs are usually deployed in groups of eight, and each member of that group has a specific function . . . be it manning the communication gear, serving as the medic, or navigating the vehicles. Each member in the group relies on and trusts the other members to do their job.

Each of us has unique abilities, gifts and talents. Some of us are musically talented, some are artistic, some can make a room of second graders do incredible things (like sit still!), some are very organized, some can teach, some are amazingly great with all sorts of people, and some can take a simple swatch of fabric and change the feel of a whole room (very impressive!). We each were given specific abilities in order to fulfill the call of God on our lives.

Because we are all so uniquely created and gifted, it is hard for me to understand why women get jealous of other women. Really, there is *no* reason. I don't need your abilities to do what it is that I am to do on this planet . . . I just have to be committed to discovering and developing the gifts within me. We are all supposed to be working together to build God's kingdom. We will do it in different ways . . . but we will all still be headed in the same direction.

So when you see someone who has a gift in a certain area, why don't you cheer her on? Rather than being bothered or threatened by her strengths, rejoice that she is on your team.

We need each other. Truly.

We are all one body, and in order for that body to function optimally, all of its parts must be doing their job. The mouth would be pathetic at trying to be the foot, and the hand would never make it as the stomach . . . and no individual part is more important than the whole.

There are no Lone Rangers in God's army. Together we are invincible. Alone we will be ineffective.

Daily Step

Of whom have you been jealous? Can you see that that emotion is a waste of time?

Day 43

She girds herself with strength [spiritual, mental and physical strength for her God-given task] and makes her arms strong and firm.

PROVERBS 31:17, *AMP*

There are things you and I are supposed to do on the planet, and we need the strength to do them! Not just physical strength . . . but mental and spiritual strength as well.

David reminds us in Psalm 92:12-13 that "the righteous shall flourish like a palm tree, He shall grow like a cedar in Lebanon. Those who are planted in the house of the LORD shall flourish in the courts of our God" (*NKJV*). David could have mentioned flourishing anywhere (school, work, home . . . the mall), but he said *in the house of God.*

Now, I don't know too much about the palm tree, but I do know that most of my spiritual strength comes from remaining deeply rooted in the house of God. A lot of people claim to love God but are trying to make it in the world on their own.

It is next to impossible to do life alone! You were not designed for it! The Church is the heart of the Father, and if we truly love Him, our heart should beat in tune with His heart for the house. No church is perfect . . . it's full of people like you and me . . . imperfect people doing the best they know how. Planting ourselves in the house is the only way to remain spiritually strong.

Planting yourself means more than just attending. It means sinking your roots in deep. It means serving. It means being a contributor, not just a consumer.

Maybe you have said at one point, "I just didn't get anything out of church today." How much did you give? Some people wake up on Sunday and say that they "just don't feel like going to church today." Well, it is not all about you! Maybe God is sending someone to your church today that *you* are supposed to encourage. Your presence is needed! The writer of Hebrews tells us not to forsake the assembling of ourselves together (see Hebrews 10:25). Church . . . some assembly required!

God's house should be extraordinary . . . abundant in life, leadership and love. It should be the most life-giving institution available to humanity. I am aware that not all churches have a firm grip on this yet, but do not give up on the heartbeat of God. Find a church that you can call home—a place where you can lay your burdens down and focus on lifting someone else's up. Find a home and plant yourself . . . because we need you strong and able—fully flourishing in the house of God.

Daily Step

Go to church this week looking for the person whom you are supposed to encourage.

Day 44

Exercise daily in God—no spiritual flabbiness, please!
Workouts in the gymnasium are useful, but a disciplined life
in God is far more so, making you fit both today and forever.

1 TIMOTHY 4:7-8, *THE MESSAGE*

I have been to the gym and have had a very muscular, abs-of-steel person show me how to use the machines. She spent quite a bit of time explaining every piece of equipment to me. She showed me exactly how to do a stomach crunch, lift a free-weight and spin on a bike. I even paid for this demonstration!

The thing is . . . all of this knowledge would get me nowhere unless I actually used the equipment. I would just get fat if all I did was look at the machines and never do a sit-up!

This is how it is for us as Christians. We have been given a lot of information on how to live a successful Christian life . . . from church, books and seminars. Some of us can quote entire chapters of the Bible. We might know the significance of the Temple or understand end-time theology. Maybe we can quote every scripture on grace and love . . . or at least know where they are in the Bible.

All of that is great. But if all we do is gain the knowledge and don't put it to use, we will just be "fat" Christians. We will have, as Paul said, "spiritual flabbiness."

A disciplined life involves putting into practice what you know . . . not just gaining more knowledge. More than just taking notes on the sermon, you should be prepared to practice what is being taught. If you are learning about forgiveness, begin to forgive! Don't just say, "That was a good sermon." Practice what you have learned. If you are reading a book about praying . . . start praying! Don't just write a book report about it.

Paul told the Corinthians that he still had to feed them "milk" (baby food); he couldn't give them solid food yet because they hadn't put into practice what they had been taught. "You are like babies as far as your faith in Christ is concerned. So I had to treat you like babies and feed you milk" (1 Corinthians 3:1-2, *CEV*).

A mature relationship with God doesn't just come by knowing more . . . it comes when we practice what we do know.

Daily Step

What have you learned this past month that you can honestly say that you haven't put into practice yet? Are you ready to do that?

Day 45

A capable, intelligent, and virtuous woman—who is he who can find her? She is far more precious than jewels and her value is far above rubies or pearls.

PROVERBS 31:10, *AMP*

Well . . . this can sound a little scary: capable, intelligent *and* virtuous?? Maybe this makes you think of all the times that you felt incapable, unintelligent and hardly a force on the earth. So what? Forget what you have felt and start right where you are. With God, you get a brand-new opportunity to expand your mental strength in order to be a force of impact and significance on the earth.

To gain mental strength, you have to swallow your pride and be willing to learn. This journey will require you to constantly be learning new things. For example, if you are getting married, are married, or planning on being married, I would suggest that you get around some awesome wives (like the ones who still have sex with their husbands!) and learn something new. And you know, kids don't exactly come with guarantees, warranties or instructions, so a few good books on parenting might be a good idea.

Are you clear on your purpose? Are you operating in that purpose? If not, discover what your passions are and learn some new things about them. If you are passionate about music, maybe you should take some lessons. If you are passionate about interior design, consider a night course that can help you grow in that skill.

Consider the career you want. If you would like a job as an editor at a publishing company and you are currently waiting tables, you have to prepare yourself now to receive that job later. Stop asking God for that new job and position yourself for Him to provide it.

Begin to retrain your mind about who you are and all the wonderful ways that you were created. The thoughts that you have been thinking about yourself have led you where you are . . . so think some new ones! Change begins with your thinking.

It is likely that WNBA star Lisa Leslie consistently asks her coach what she can do to improve her game. What makes us any different? And when we are given a new direction, we should avoid being defensive and act on that direction. Change makes us stretch . . . but that is just what we need after a good workout.

Daily Step

What new thing have you learned this week? What book are you reading?

Day 46

Show me how you work, GOD; School me in your ways.

PSALM 25:4, *THE MESSAGE*

Study and be eager and do your utmost to present yourself to God approved (tested by trial), a workman who has no cause to be ashamed, correctly analyzing and accurately dividing [rightly handling and skillfully teaching] the Word of Truth.

2 TIMOTHY 2:15, *AMP*

---

stud·y *n.* to apply oneself to learning

Maybe you are still in school working toward a degree or a diploma. Good for you. Finish!

However, I would like to suggest that each of us should see ourselves as being in school. We may not be sitting behind a desk or looking at a chalkboard, but until we step out of this life, we should consider ourselves students.

In fact, we could step out of this life sooner if we stop learning. Valerie Monroe, the beauty director for *O, The Oprah Magazine,* states, "Though it was once believed the brain was incapable of regenerating new cells throughout life, researchers have recently found that, at least in some areas, regeneration does occur; and that staying mentally active can cause the brain to sprout new connections between nerve cells."[4] This means that we will live longer and better if we continue to learn.

You and I have an obligation to hand the "baton" that we are currently running with over to a younger generation. We won't even finish our lap of this race if we are not learning new things. What I have learned thus far has gotten me to this point in my race, but if I am to finish strong, I must continue to learn.

So go ahead and learn to speak Italian, learn to repair a car engine, learn the benefits of wheatgrass, or learn how to graph differential equations (!). All of that knowledge will cause your brain to be stronger! Just make sure that in all of your learning you allow yourself to be schooled in the ways of your God. Make sure that you are reading His Word and studying a portion of it regularly. Be in a church where God's Word is being taught. Be an *A* student in knowing all about your God.

Daily Step

Proverbs 18:15 states, "Wise men and women are always learning, always listening for fresh insights (THE MESSAGE). What does this verse say to you?

Summing it all up, friends, I'd say you'll do best by filling your minds and meditating on things true, noble, reputable, authentic, compelling, gracious—the best, not the worst; the beautiful, not the ugly; thing to praise, not things to curse. Put into practice what you've learned from me, what you heard and saw and realized.

PHILIPPIANS 4:8-9, *THE MESSAGE*

Half empty . . . half full . . . half empty . . . half full . . . which kind of person would you say that you are?

Just because I smile and laugh a lot (and I am blond) does not mean that I am living far off in dreamland. I am aware of reality. Although my husband is wonderful, he is not perfect. It is my choice to decide what to see—all the things he is not doing right according to me, or all the great things that make me love him so much.

I have two very strong-willed children . . . teenage children . . . and sometimes it is hard to even relate to what they might be thinking. Instead of focusing on what I would like them to do and say, I have to focus on drawing the best out of them—and there is plenty to draw out!

On a daily basis (sometimes a moment-by-moment basis), I have to choose to see the glass half full. Having a positive attitude and perspective helps us achieve the possibilities we see before us.

It is possible to have an amazing marriage and to raise children who are about the Father's business, but it will never come from focusing on the negative—which most people do. Optimism should be part of our makeup, despite the fact that we are bombarded with negativity.

> A pessimist sees only the dark side of the clouds, and mopes; a philosopher sees both sides, and shrugs; an optimist doesn't see the clouds at all—he's walking on them.
>
> —Leonard Louis Levinson

Yes, champions develop mental strength, and this certainly includes our intelligence. However, equally (if not more) important is our ability to control the direction that our thoughts take. You may not be able to control the first thought that pops into your head, but you can control the second and the third.

Daily Step

What lovely, noble or gracious thing can you think on today?

Day 48

*Are God's promises not enough for you, spoken so
gently and tenderly? Why do you let your emotions
take over, lashing out and spitting fire.*

JOB 15:11-12, *THE MESSAGE*

I can look back on a few (that is my code word for "a lot") times in my life when I reacted from an emotional place. For instance, one time I yelled at my son . . . no, really . . . *yelled!* Not okay. Even though my son had done something to make me angry, I was definitely overreacting. I recognized at that point that there had to be another reason I was lashing out at him. As I was sorting through my feelings, I realized some other things had happened that day at work . . . with my friend . . . and I had not resolved any of it. Unfortunately, because I had not dealt with my emotions earlier in the day, my son had to bear the brunt of more than his own misbehavior.[5]

Controlling your emotions sometimes means that you do exactly the opposite of what you feel. There are a lot of very brilliant people who cannot achieve the success that they are capable of achieving simply because they cannot control their emotions. When they are upset, they wilt; when they are angry, they make everyone around them suffer. When they are frustrated, they can't accomplish their job. You cannot justify bad behavior just because you "felt like it."

It is easy to fall into bad habits when you are led by your emotions.

"I don't *feeeeel* like working out."

"I don't *feeeeel* like waiting for God to bring the right man for me."

"I don't *feeeeel* like loving my husband."

"I don't *feeeeel* like dealing with my children."

Well, duh!

Who "feeeels" like it all the time? But if bad habits are formed by our emotions, shouldn't the opposite also be true? Let your emotions fuel some good habits. Chat with a girlfriend, go for a walk, take a bubble bath . . . or how about thinking about the long-term consequences of your action before you take it? Mental strength starts with controlling your emotions.

Our emotions are a gift. How awesome it is to simply *feel* joy, excitement, sadness . . . whatever. We just can't let the emotion take over. We can't pay bills, or parent, or work when we *feel* like it. Nope, we have to do the right thing . . . oftentimes in spite of how we are feeling.

C'mon . . . you can do it . . . you champion, you!

Daily Step

Is there someone you need to apologize to? Someone who had to bear the brunt of your runaway emotion?

So if you're serious about living this new resurrection life with Christ, act like it. Pursue the things over which Christ presides. Don't shuffle along, eyes to the ground, absorbed with the things right in front of you. Look up, and be alert to what is going on around Christ—that's where the action is. See things from his perspective.

COLOSSIANS 3:1-2, *THE MESSAGE*

Sadly, I had to buy reading glasses a few years ago. I tried to find really cute ones at least . . . but they were still glasses! What was amazing was how clear the page I was reading in a book became once I put them on. The words were suddenly in focus and very easy to read. Interestingly, I really hadn't realized that the words were out of focus until I put the glasses on and experienced true clarity.

Sometimes I think that is how we live each day . . . not quite in focus. Or perhaps we focus on the wrong things. At times, we can be so shortsighted that we miss what is all around us. What are you focusing on? I have found that I tend to head toward what I am focusing on.

Jesus visited His disciples one time by walking on the water. Peter thought that was pretty cool, so he asked Jesus if he could do it too. Jesus said, "Come on, Peter." Peter stepped out of the boat (that took courage!) and walked toward Jesus. He was doing fine until he took his eyes off Jesus and focused on the stormy sea. When Peter's focus changed, he began to sink.

What are you focusing on? Building a great marriage? Then you can't let the challenge that you might be facing today keep you from focusing on the marriage you want.

What are you focusing on? Financial freedom? Then you need to stay focused on a budget that will help you get there (in spite of the cute shoes you just saw at the mall!! ☺).

What are you focusing on? That degree from a university? Then you might have to skip that party and study.

What are you focusing on? Helping someone else? Then you might have to look past her weaknesses and help anyway.

What are you focusing on? Getting through a challenge? Then you might have to take your eyes off of the wind and the waves and focus on what God has done for you. He has seen you through all sorts of tough times. He will see you through this one, too. Don't focus on the storm: Focus on Him and His promises to you.

Daily Step

Read Hebrews 12:1-3.
Where are you fixing your eyes?

Day 50

You've all been to the stadium and seen the athletes race. Everyone runs; one wins. Run to win. All good athletes train hard. They do it for a gold medal that tarnishes and fades. You're after one that's gold eternally. I don't know about you, but I'm running hard for the finish line. I'm giving it everything I've got. No sloppy living for me!

1 CORINTHIANS 9:24-26, *THE MESSAGE*

I'm sure that Venus and Serena Williams, who are both awesome athletes, have had to focus on training and gaining strength and ability. That involves rigorous training: exercising daily, following a strict diet, taking the best supplements, and resting the right amount of time.

You are equally as valuable as any great athlete, and you also are in constant training. Exercise your body and your mind and put the stuff in your body that will help it, not hurt it. We need you to live a long and healthy life!

After being diagnosed with cancer, I took a long look at how I was "training." I soon realized that there were some definite changes that I needed to make if I was going to run my race to win. I may not be able to control the quality of air I breathe, but I can control what I put in my mouth. I can control how much exercise I get. I now eat *a lot* of raw green stuff (!), take great supplements, and exercise every day.

The truth is, I never *feel* like exercising . . . but I do it anyway—even right now, in the midst of radiation treatments. I would also much rather have a cheeseburger and banana split, but instead I choose salmon and a salad. Why? Because I am in training. "No sloppy living for me!"

As champion athletes, we should watch not only what is going into our mouths but also what we ingest through our eyes and ears. I love movies, but I don't just go out and see every movie that is made. I enjoy people, but I have to watch who I spend my time with.

The people you spend your time with will affect you, so be careful that you don't surround yourself with negative people who will influence your awesome attitude. Listen to music . . . it's awesome, but be careful about which music you listen to. There is a lot of junk in our world that might interfere with you finishing your race strong. Don't let that happen![6]

I do these things because I have an obligation to my Creator to finish the race that He has set me on. You do too.

Daily Step

What can you improve about your diet? Are you getting the right kind of exercise? Are you setting yourself up to live a long life? How?

Day 51

For you have need of steadfast patience and endurance,
so that you may perform and fully accomplish the
will of God, and thus receive and carry away
[and enjoy to the full] what is promised.

HEBREWS 10:36, *AMP*

Confession time again! One of the weaknesses that I noticed about myself a few years ago was that I didn't always finish the projects that I started. I am a great starter . . . it's just my finishing that needs work! As soon as a project got a little mundane or slightly boring, I would quit, rationalize my decision (why should I have to put up with boring??), and then look for something more exciting. (I am much better at finishing now, but I'm still a work in progress!)

Here's a tip for free . . . sometimes life, marriage and work *are* boring . . . or at least just routine. Because we are grown-ups, our decisions during those times actually say a lot about our character.

You can't just quit now (I know, I know . . . stop whining). God has a purpose in everything He does, and there is certainly a reason for this "boring" season in your life.

Why don't you find new ways to make the routine interesting . . . buy someone a coffee while standing in line or talk to someone in the elevator (that always makes for hilarious expressions) . . . whatever you do, don't give up! You'll miss the fun stuff if you quit now!

Divorce is at an all-time high in our nation. We fall in love with falling in love (say that 10 times fast) and we always want something new and exciting. Instead of a lifetime's worth of amazing memories, we want excitement. The reality is that roses don't come every day and once you are married, the wooing is not quite like it was in the honeymoon phase. Sometimes you will even wonder who the heck you married, but you don't quit just because its not "new." You have to make it new!

If things seem boring, maybe you have something to do with it . . . just a thought. Finish what you start. Don't quit when it's boring . . . focus on what is ahead and the kind of life that you would like to look back on.

I have been sent to this planet not just to start the race but also to finish it . . . and finish strong. My Creator doesn't get glory in what I start; He gets glory in what I finish. So in spite of difficulty or boredom . . . I will finish what I have started. How about you?

Champions persevere.

per·se·ver·ance *n.* steady persistence in adhering to a course of action

Daily Step

What is one thing that you started but didn't finish? Can you finish it?

Day 52

*You are better off to have a friend than to be all alone,
because then you will get more enjoyment out of what you
earn. If you fall, your friend can help you up. But if you fall
without having a friend nearby, you are really in trouble.*

ECCLESIASTES 4:9-10, CEV

friend *n.* a person whom one knows, likes, and trusts

You and I were not created to live out the journey of life alone.
We were designed for companionship . . . for friendship. If we
are going to fulfill what we were created to fulfill, we will do it by
staying connected to the people who join us in life. We were not
created to solve all life's problems on our own. We do not have
all the answers. We need each other.

I had a very sad conversation with someone the other day.
She is in the midst of a serious health challenge . . . she is basically fighting for her life. I had not met this woman before, but
someone suggested that I call her . . . so I did. When she
picked up the phone, one of the first things out of her mouth
was, "I am so afraid. I am all alone." That broke my heart,
because no one should have to go through what this woman is
going through all on her own. I quickly mobilized some of my

friends, and we brought her into our world.

So, how did she get that way?

She chose it.

I know that sounds harsh, but the only way we could possibly be alone is if we have made a series of decisions that have led to our aloneness. While this woman was busy doing other things, people were exiting her world. While she was busy with her life, she gave no time to connect with the right kind of people . . . the people who stick with you through the good and the bad.

And now she is alone. Well, actually, not anymore . . . because we have invaded! There are girls going to her house, driving her to the doctor, praying for her . . . basically just being her friends. She can no longer say that she is alone.

Don't let the busyness of life cause you to neglect the value of friends. So many things pull at our time, and if we are not careful, we will find ourselves spending little to no time with the friends whom God has sent to join us on life's adventure. I believe that the friendships we build are so important—not only for our happiness, but also for our success in life.

Daily Step

Which friend can you call today . . . just to check in? How about sending that person a card?

Day 53

*He comes alongside us when we go through hard times,
and before you know it, he brings us alongside someone else
who is going through hard times so that we can be there for
that person just as God was there for us.*

2 CORINTHIANS 1:4-5, *THE MESSAGE*

*Older women . . . are to give good counsel and be
teachers of what is right and noble.*

TITUS 2:3, *AMP*

---

old·er *adj:* skilled or able through long experience; practiced

It doesn't matter how old you are right now or how many candles were on your last birthday cake. You are an older woman. Why? . . . because there is someone younger than you on the planet. And as long as there is someone younger than you, you are an older woman.

Before you frown at me, let me assure you that older is good. And all of us, whether we are 16 or 96, have an obligation to be an example to someone younger. As Paul put it, we are to "give good counsel and be teachers of what is right and noble." We are to be willing to be an example of what to do . . . what not to do . . . and how to do it.

You probably have had to overcome serious challenges in your lifetime. There are plenty of women who need your help to go through the same things that you have been through. Wouldn't you have loved someone to help you on your journey?

You could have been a victim of sexual abuse . . . just like three out of every four women. Now, that is a scary statistic—and it means that a young woman in your world probably needs your help to get healing.

Marriage can be pretty tough at times, and there are younger women watching you as you navigate through yours. She needs to know what you know! Find yourself a young, sassy single and help her understand her value so that she will make wise choices about whom she marries. If you raised teenagers (and are still alive), rope a younger mom into your world and teach her what you have learned . . . so that she doesn't have to learn the hard way.

Maybe you have been able to buy your own home. I'll bet there is someone who needs to hear how to clean up her credit and how to get herself in a position to purchase her own home. Everything that you have endured in your past can benefit someone else's future . . . but you must be willing to invest in people. Invest your wisdom into the soil of a younger woman's heart and you will always find yourself profiting along the way.

Daily Step

What piece of costly wisdom would you be willing to share with a younger woman? Can you think of a younger woman you could extend a hand to?

Day 54

Oil and perfume rejoice the heart; so does the sweetness of a friend's counsel that comes from the heart.

PROVERBS 27:9, AMP

---

loy·al *adj:* steadfast in allegiance, unwavering in devotion

A loyal friend is worth her weight in gold . . . maybe more. Can I be a friend who is "steadfast in allegiance"?

Loyalty does not equal convenience . . . who knew? We cannot be the kind of people who are loyal until something better comes along. We cannot ditch old friends for new ones just because they can do more for us than the old ones can.

Loyalty means being committed in the tough times . . . I mean the really hard times, when you are emotionally exhausted just from listening! Relationships are not 50/50 (if only we could be so lucky). Just like marriage, there are times when it is 80/20 . . . or even 100/0! The difficult times yield the most satisfying relational moments. They teach you that you are loved . . . even in the hard times . . . even when you are a mess . . . even when you don't want to get up in the morning. If that is how God loves us, then the least we can do is love our friends the same way. Loyalty is not only enduring the difficult times; it is loving your friends *in* those difficult times.[7]

However, oftentimes it is harder for us to be loyal when things are going great in a friend's life. Paul tells us in the book of Romans that not only are we to mourn with our friends when they mourn, but we are to rejoice with them when they rejoice. What if something happens to your friend that you wish would happen to you? Can you rejoice with her then?

Can you be happy for your friend who is getting a promotion . . . when you yourself have wanted to advance in your career for months?? Can you be happy for your friend who is getting married or got a great promotion . . . again . . . and you really want both of those? And if you are the married or promoted one, can you cut your friend some slack as she works on rejoicing with you?

Daily Step

Is there someone that you have pulled away from simply because she is going through a hard time . . . and you are tired of listening? Or is there someone you have pulled away from because you are finding it hard to rejoice with her? Can you contact that friend today?

Day 55

And these God-chosen lives all around—
what splendid friends they make!

PSALM 16:3, *THE MESSAGE*

Normally, I am not that crazy about putting together a puzzle. I am more of an action girl. But something happens around Christmas time when my parents come to visit. We start one of those million-piece puzzles . . . OK . . . it's not a million pieces . . . but it feels like it! And because the puzzle is there, I slow down enough to put my share of the pieces in and just visit with my parents.

The many pieces in a puzzle reminds me of friendship. Every friend has a different role in our lives and a different shape in our hearts, and each friend takes a different size piece in our hearts. There are acquaintances, people we work with, friends and our intimate friends . . . the sisters of our hearts.

All relationships start out as acquaintances, the small pieces in the puzzle . . . and then some make the journey toward intimate friendship. Obviously, we need to respect the different characteristics of our friends, such as taste and style . . . learning to find the joy and humor in them (I mean, how could she like *those* plaid pants!?) . . . but our intimate friends will have the same (or very similar) core values as us. They may not be expressed the same way, but the heart of each issue will be similar. For example, if honesty were a core value of yours, it would be hard to be a friend with someone who regularly lies about everything.

When I look at the puzzle of friendship that represents my world, I smile. There are so many different kinds of people represented . . . so many different size pieces. I love that!

Unlike real puzzles, the pieces in your friendship puzzle will change sizes. Some might become smaller, while some will grow bigger. You need to have a heart that lets people come and go. Always keep your life open for friends, because you could meet one of the best friends you will ever have next week! I'm sure that you have been hurt and possibly betrayed a time or two by friends. Yes, that hurts. But don't allow the hurt to become bitterness. Bitterness will cause you to close your heart to people.

Friends, who *all* start out just as acquaintances, are truly one of heaven's best gifts to you!

Daily Step

What does your puzzle look like?
Can you think of a few acquaintances or
people you work with who are on the journey
toward being an intimate friend?
What will it take?

Day 56

*Jacob said . . . "When I saw your face, it was
as the face of God smiling on me."*

GENESIS 33:10, *THE MESSAGE*

There have been so many moments when the face of my friends brightened my day, brought me hope, or made me laugh. I can only pray that my face has done the same for them.

I have spent a number of hours with my friends in airport lounges (before 9/11 . . . when they used to let you into the airport as a nonpassenger!) when they had a layover at the Los Angeles airport. Getting to the airport was always a nightmare, but the joy of connecting with my friends was well worth it.

My friend Shanelle flew from her home in Denmark to go with me to one of my many doctor's appointments this year. My friend Bobbie came from Australia to be with me in the hospital. And let me tell you, when I saw their faces . . . my world brightened.

There are some friends in my life who are supposed to be forever friends, so I do whatever it takes to maintain the friendship. To maintain or to build a relationship takes time. And there are a lot of creative ways to do that. One of my friends gets together with some women every other month in a book club. Some get together every week to exercise. Some get together and cook. Some connect at a Bible study.

It is a new day for us women, and I love that we have so many opportunities that the generations before us never had. We can vote . . . we can have any career we want . . . we don't have to attend barn raisings (although I am sure they were fun) . . . we have hair dryers and lipstick.

op·por·tu·ni·ty *n:* a favorable or advantageous circumstance or combination of circumstances; a favorable or suitable occasion or time

But with so many of us attempting to balance life (work, kids, husband, house, school), connecting with our friends can get difficult. Sometimes we let it fall through the cracks instead of giving our friendship the time and effort it takes to be forever friends. You have planted some seeds with the women in your life . . . now go water them! That is probably all those seeds need to grow.

Daily Step

Send another card to a different friend!
Tell her one way that her friendship has
made a difference in your world.

Get along among yourselves, each of you doing your part . . .
Be patient with each person, attentive to individual needs.
And be careful that when you get on each other's nerves you
don't snap at each other. Look for the best in each other,
and always do your best to bring it out.

1 THESSALONIANS 5:13-15, *THE MESSAGE*

Have you ever been with someone who just makes you like yourself more when you are with her? She just seems to bring out the best in you. She laughs at your jokes and thinks your stories are awesome. She enjoys every moment with you.

On the other hand, have you been with someone who . . . and it doesn't matter what you do . . . you just can't seem to do anything right? She seems to barely tolerate you.

We probably all have had both of those experiences. Of those two people, which one would you rather be with? The one who celebrates you . . . or the one who tolerates you?

Duh . . . we all like to be celebrated. This probably isn't going to happen with everyone you meet, though.

Thinking about this question made me ask myself . . . *Do I celebrate people? Or do I just tolerate them?*

Remember the cheerleaders' chant in Junior High: "Two, four, six, eight . . . who do we appreciate!" When did we stop saying that cheer?? We all like to be appreciated. Can we still be a little cheerleader-like?

Now, I am aware that some people just get on your nerves. The apostle Paul was even aware of this. He simply cautions us that when it happens . . . to not snap at each other.

When you are with someone, look for ways to celebrate her. Is there anything great about her that you can focus on? Remind yourself that she is also a loved daughter of the King and that your Father wants you to be looking for the best in her.

I am not saying that this will be easy, because as soon as someone gets on your nerves, all of the things about her that bother you will seem to pile up. And it gets hard to find anything good.

Well . . . try. If she is not a believer, your kindness might very well lead her to the Father. And if she is a believer, your love for her will be a testimony to others who are watching.

Daily Step

During the next conversation you have with a friend, work at bringing out the best in her!

Day 58

*You hear, O LORD, the desire of the afflicted; you
encourage them, and you listen to their cry.*

PSALM 10:17, *NIV*

Listen to my prayer, O God, do not ignore my plea.

PSALM 55:1, *NIV*

lis·ten *v:* to make an effort to hear something

"How's it going?" I asked my friend.

"Oh . . . fine," she replied.

"What are your plans for the holidays?" I continued.

"Ummm . . . not exactly sure yet," she responded.

This was a seemingly insignificant, everyday kind of conversation. And if I hadn't been listening . . . not just hearing sound come out of my friend's mouth, but really listening . . . I might have walked away thinking nothing of it. I would have thought she was just unsure but had lots of options.

But I heard something in my friend's voice that made me want to pursue the conversation and ask more questions. Eventually, she told me she had just had a conversation with her mother that hadn't gone very well. She cried as she told me of her hurt and bafflement over a relationship gone sour.

Listening requires effort. Listening requires us to focus on someone other than ourselves.

We have the promise that God listens to us. He makes an effort to hear the cry of our heart . . . not just the cry of our lips. He listens for every nuance, every tone of our voice. Thank You, God.

To the best of our ability, you and I are to do the same. We are to be great listeners. Compassionate listeners. Active listeners. Listening requires 100 percent of our attention. It requires that we turn off our cell phones, turn down the music, and look at the person who is sharing her heart.

I have been guilty so many times of thinking that if I heard what the person was saying, I was listening. Not true. Listening involves more than simply repeating what we have heard . . . it means understanding the heart of the person who said it.

Let's be friends who listen.

Daily Step

Shhhhhh . . . let someone else talk and share . . . you just listen.

Day 59

So, chosen by God for this new life of love, dress in the wardrobe God picked out for you: compassion, kindness, humility, quiet strength, discipline. Be even-tempered, content with second place, quick to forgive an offense.

COLOSSIANS 3:12-13, *THE MESSAGE*

Some of my friends are just weird.

And I have learned to like that about them! ☺

I guess what makes them weird is that they are different from me. When I look around at my ever-increasing circle of friends, I notice that most of them are different from me. And the truth is that my life is richer because they are.

I didn't always think this way, however. It sounds good to say, "You should be building relationships with people who are different from you. . . people with different personalities and strengths." But acting that out of can be a bit tricky.

In your friendship circle, you probably have someone who is the "party in a bottle" person. She is the outgoing, talkative one who has a hard time finishing anything . . . unless it is your sentence!

And you probably know the "ducks in a row" person. This is the friend who likes everything perfect and organized, the one whose checkbook is always balanced. And when things don't go perfectly (and when does that happen??), she can get depressed.

I am sure you are also acquainted with the girl who has goals for every occasion. She freely expresses her opinion and will tell you yours if you are quiet for five seconds. She keeps the group moving and on target.

And, of course you know the girl who is soooo peaceful. She likes everybody and hates conflict. She patiently listens to your tales of woe over and over. She doesn't like change, however, so you'd better give her plenty of notice if you are going to alter the plans. Your life is better because you have people with different personalities in it. Not always easier . . . but better.

As friends, let's value not only the friendship but also the person. There is just something spectacular about hanging out with someone who shows she is enjoying being with you. One of the ways that we show we value our friends is to love who they really are. Love the differences between you and your friends that rise so glaringly to the surface. Don't just accept them, but love them.

Be good friends who love deeply.

Daily Step

What do you think when you read the following quote from Carl Rogers:

When I walk on the beach to watch the sunset, I do not call out, "A little more orange over to the right, please," or "Would you mind giving us less purple in the back?" No, I enjoy the always-different sunsets as they are. We do well to do the same with people we love.[8]

*So—join the company of good men and women,
keep your feet on the tried and true paths. It's the men
who walk straight who will settle this land, the women
with integrity who will last here.*

PROVERBS 2:20-21, *THE MESSAGE*

Most of us have a dream in our heart—or at least we did at one point. Maybe the challenges of life have quieted the dream that was once beating strongly within you. We all need a friend with whom we can share that dream so that when it seems as if the dream might not come to pass, she can continue to offer encouragement.

Without the encouragement of my friends, there are many things that I would have given up on (marriage, black belt, first book). But my friends couldn't have encouraged me it I hadn't opened my heart and shared its secrets . . . dreams as well as fears.

Sometimes we try so hard to be independent. We really weren't created to live independently; we were created to live interdependently . . . linked to each other. And this happens only when we are willing to be intimate. So let's get real!

We need to get over our fear of betrayal so that we can open our hearts. One thing that keeps us from opening our hearts to others is the fear of being hurt or let down. If you are alive, you have probably been betrayed. I haven't met anyone who hasn't been.

Yes, we should be wise about how and to whom we share our heart (like . . . don't share too much too fast . . . let the person prove faithful in the little you share before you give them more), but we do need to open up. There are ways to provide opportunities for intimacy (eating together, working on a project together), but true intimacy involves communication. "Talk is the currency of friendship. The route to sympathy, understanding and connection is through talk."[9]

Talking . . . listening . . . encouraging . . . challenging . . . talking . . . listening . . . encouraging . . . challenging . . . talking . . . listening . . . and it keeps on going.

Remind your friend on a regular basis how much you love her. Remind her that she is loyal and that you are thankful you can depend on her. Trust her with the dreams in your heart. Talk to her about your deepest fears. Send her a card, an e-mail, talk over coffee . . . just start communicating.

Daily Step

Read Proverbs 27:17. What does this verse say to you?

Day 61

Reliable friends who do what they say are like cool drinks in sweltering heat—refreshing!

PROVERBS 25:13, *THE MESSAGE*

Just as lotions and fragrance give sensual delight, a sweet friendship refreshes the soul.

PROVERBS 27:9, *THE MESSAGE*

I think it is so cool that God, knowing the purpose for which He created me, has sent people to join with me on this journey. He knows me, so He continually sends people with strengths to help me in my weaknesses. He knows my every thought, so He sends people to help me process those thoughts. He knows the weapons that the enemy might throw my way, so He sends fellow warriors to help me hold my shield and swing my sword. He knows the gifts and talents that He has given me, so He opens doors and provides opportunities for me to use those gifts and talents to help others.

In the same way, God sends me into the lives of others to join with them on their journey. He knows my strengths, so He sends me to help someone in her weakness. He knows my thoughts, so He sends me to help someone navigate her thoughts. He knows me, so He sends me to help someone hold her shield and lift her sword. He knows the gifts and talents that He has given me, so He sends me to help others along their journey.

All that I have done is to stay on the path that He has set out for me to the best of my ability . . . this life path that will accomplish His will. As I have done this, countless numbers of people have become friends. Relationships have been built that have been instrumental in helping me fulfill God's will, and which have also been important in helping my friend fulfill His will.

It is so important for you to keep walking the path that God set you upon. There are people in your future who are counting on meeting you. Their destiny is linked to yours. You will never fulfill the purpose for which God has created you on your own. You need those heaven-sent people in your world today, and you will need them tomorrow, next year, and in 20 years to come.

Thank God that He, in His wisdom, saw fit to connect us to amazing people. You are not alone.

Daily Step

Think of the people who have come across your path at just the right time to help you through something. Can you think of an instance when God sent you across someone else's path at the moment when she really needed you?

Day 62

Give your entire attention to what God is doing right now, and don't get worked up about what may or may not happen tomorrow. God will help you deal with whatever hard things come up when the time comes.

MATTHEW 6:34, *THE MESSAGE*

---

now *adv:* at the present time

Now.

In the present.

Are you here? Or are you so busy looking at the future that you are not living in your now moment? Are you so preoccupied with what might happen that you are not aware of what is actually happening?

We all have unique talents and abilities. We have differences . . . you, for example, may be able to sing through a whole song—in key (it's hardly fair). We all grew up in different neighborhoods with different economic backgrounds, full of different dreams in our hearts. But the one thing we all have in common is 24 hours. We all are responsible for the 24 hours of this day . . . and it starts with now.

Sometimes we mess up our now moments by not living in them. While we are at work, we wonder if we took care of everything at home this morning. And while we are at home, we worry about that project we left unfinished at the office.

We have got to learn to live in the moment, where we are.

For six weeks this past year, I got radiation treatments almost every day. I would show up at the radiation oncology center at the same time every day. At first I was just a bit (!) resentful that I even needed to do this. I didn't want the cancer, and I certainly did not want the radiation. I saw the whole thing as one big imposition.

Then one day, I made the decision that since I was going to be at the oncology center, I might as well take advantage of the moments that I had with the other people who were there. After making that decision, I began talking to the other cancer patients in the room . . . many of whom were very scared and feeling very alone. I handed out books and just tried to share the life and love of God with my new friends. Rather than wishing I wasn't there, I began to be fully present in the moment.

Your turn. Live in the moment that you have been given. Now.

Daily Step

Today, try to be conscious and present in every moment. If the line you are standing in at the store is long, enjoy the book that you brought along. If the traffic on the freeway is horrible, enjoy the song on the radio. If your baby wakes you up at 2 A.M., enjoy the moment of holding a precious life.

Day 63

Happiness makes a person smile, but sadness can break a person's spirit

PROVERBS 15:13, NCV

hap·pi·ness *n:* characterized by cheerfulness; willingness

So many of us put off being happy. When we were 4 we could hardly wait to go to kindergarten, and then when we were 12 we were impatient to begin junior high.

And of course, our life would be great once we got into high school, and then it would be amazing once we graduated . . . got into college . . . got married . . . had children . . . got a promotion . . . got divorced . . . found a new husband . . . got a face-lift . . . had grandchildren . . . retired . . . and the list of waiting to be happy goes on and on.

Looking forward to something is important, but don't let it overshadow the value of today.

I work hard at trying to see each day as an adventure in itself. Yes, I am looking forward to the day when I no longer have to talk to my radiation oncologist . . . but in the meantime, I am enjoying the new people that I am meeting and the opportunities to make a difference in someone's life.

I am excited about the few days that my husband and I are going to take off in the next month . . . but I can't wait until then to be happy. I will be thrilled when my daughter no longer has science projects to complete . . . but in the meantime I will enjoy (or really try to!!) learning about stuff I never thought I would.

I would like to suggest that happiness is a choice. I know, this sounds way too simple. But it's true. Your happiness does not rely on your circumstances changing but on you changing how you see your circumstances.

Go ahead and put on your happy face!! ☺

Daily Step

Make the decision that today is a great one and that you are going to enjoy all the adventure of it! (Don't forget to smile . . . remember, the rest of us are looking at your face!)

Day 64

In the Messiah, in Christ, God leads us from place to place in one perpetual victory parade. Through us, he brings knowledge of Christ. Everywhere we go, people breath in the exquisite fragrance. Because of Christ, we give off a sweet scent rising to God, which is recognized by those on the way to salvation.

2 CORINTHIANS 2:14-15, *THE MESSAGE*

I love the thought that every day I am walking in a parade. Bring on the band and the confetti!!

Jesus paid a tremendous price at the cross for you and me to walk in victory. We are not fighting *for* victory. We are living *from a place of* victory. Christ made us victorious. Maybe we should live like it!

Let's find a reason to celebrate! Birthdays and anniversaries are obvious times to celebrate, but let's not forget to celebrate the smaller victories.

Did you finish that algebra class? Yippee!

Did you and your husband survive a home renovation? Yea!

Did you find the perfect dress for your daughter's wedding? Hooray!

Did you lose those 15 pounds? Have a party!

Is it a beautiful day outside? Smile!

Are you healthy? Throw some confetti!

And the list goes on . . .

There is something contagious about laughter. It is hard to frown or even to remain untouched when someone is really laughing. I always want to be where the laughter . . . the celebration . . . the life . . . is.

> A person without a sense of humor is like a wagon without springs, jolted by every pebble in the road.
> —Henry Ward Beecher

Your parade attitude is contagious and will affect any room you walk into . . . just like your bitter, angry attitude will influence those around you. Why don't you develop the reputation for being the cheerful parade person . . . the one who is continually looking for moments to celebrate?

Daily Step

Who in your world would be affected by your confetti-throwing parade attitude?

Day 65

Consider it pure joy, my brothers, whenever you face trials of many kinds, because you know that the testing of your faith develops perseverance. Perseverance must finish its work so that you may be mature and complete, not lacking anything.

JAMES 1:2-4, *NIV*

OK . . . so if we want to be "mature and complete," we need to learn how to find joy in the midst of difficulties. Most of us can smile when things are going our way, but can we do the same in the middle of a trial?

You might be facing a trial or challenge right now. If you are, I am sorry. If I were there, I would give you a great big hug. At some point, however, I would remind you that you can get through this time. God's promise of strength is for you right now. And I would encourage you to dig deep for the joy that is your strength.

In Nehemiah 8, Ezra was reading the Word of God to the Israelites, and they were overwhelmed. Perhaps this was because they understood the majesty of God for the first time, or perhaps it was because they understood that they were loved. Regardless, they were weeping. But Nehemiah snapped them out of that mood by telling them to go celebrate . . . to eat good food and to give presents to those who don't have anything good to eat:

Then Nehemiah the governor, Ezra the priest and scribe, and the Levites who were interpreting for the people said to them, "Don't weep on such a day as this! For today is a sacred day before the LORD your God." All the people had been weeping as they listened to the words of the law.

And Nehemiah continued, "Go and celebrate with a feast of choice foods and sweet drinks, and share gifts of food with people who have nothing prepared. This is a sacred day before our Lord. Don't be dejected and sad, for the joy of the LORD is your strength!" (vv. 9-10, *NLT*).

Nehemiah was telling the Israelites . . . and us . . . to let go of our sadness, because the joy of the Lord is our strength.

In the midst of your challenge, is there anything you can celebrate? If you need strength to get through it . . . and I would bet you do . . . then you must realize that your strength comes from joy. Joy is a decision, not a feeling. Joy will also involve giving to others. In the midst of your challenge, joy will be made real to you as you seek to give to someone else.

Daily Step

OK, I know this is not easy . . . but in the middle of the challenge that you are facing, can you make a list of the things that you are thankful for? Can you celebrate the fact that this trial is making you stronger?

Day 66

*One final word, friends. We ask you—urge is more like it—
that you keep on doing what we told you to do to please God,
not in a dogged religious plod, but in a living, spirited dance.
You know the guidelines we laid out for you from the
Master Jesus. God wants you to live a pure life.*

1 THESSALONIANS 4:1-2, *THE MESSAGE*

A few years ago, I sat next to a gentleman on an airplane who asked me what I did for a living. There are just sooo many answers I have for that question! I am a wife, mother, teacher, pastor . . . on this particular day, however, I decided to go with the answer of pastor. He was shocked (wonder why??).

The man actually laughed at first, and then said, "No, really . . . what do you do?" When I assured him that indeed I was a pastor, he had a hard time gelling his concept of what a pastor looked and acted like . . . and me. He said that I just seemed too alive, too happy to be a pastor.

The man's image of a church leader was that of a very somber, lifeless person. Actually, that made me sad. I almost felt that I needed to apologize to him for the impression that others had perhaps given him. Loving God should make us the most alive people on the earth!

Some people think that following God means that we are to live a blah, beige life. Some people think that if you truly love God, you can't have too much fun. I think loving God should put a twinkle in our eye. I think loving God should cause us to be filled with laughter on a regular basis.

Our walk with God should not be a "dogged religious plod." We are not supposed to be dragging our feet, wearing droopy faces or saying, "following God is so hard." *No!!* Our journey with God is lived out in a "living, spirited dance"!

Maybe we need to take dancing lessons. Really. So go put on your dancing shoes and have a ☺ day! You should be living a life that is so contagious with the joy of God that people want what you have!

Daily Step

How do you see your journey with God? Is it hard? Or is it filled with wonder and hope? How can you make it more of an adventure?

Day 67

*Be cheerful no matter what; pray all the time' thank
God no matter what happens. This is the way God wants
you who belong to Christ Jesus to live.*

1 THESSALONIANS 5:16-18, *THE MESSAGE*

---

cheer·ful *adj:* promoting a feeling of cheer; pleasant

Years ago, I was in a creative think-tank meeting that included a panel of women whom I had never met before. We had a great time talking about different subjects and sharing ideas. It was an energetic group of women who were quick thinkers and who could articulate their thoughts very well.

One of the women was a little quieter than the rest of us, but her comments and thoughts were amazing. After the meeting, I complemented her on the ideas and thoughts that she had shared. She was a little surprised that I was taking the time to complement her. She thanked me and walked away with a smile on her face. So did I.

I am not sure how you are feeling right at this moment. But if you are a little low on the cheerful scale, then perhaps you should give some cheer away. God has promised us that we will reap what we sow. If we give away a little cheer . . . it will come back to us.

Proverbs 18:21 states, "The tongue has the power of life and death, and those who love it will eat its fruit" (*NIV*). Our words are powerful tools that can bring hurt or healing. With our words we can either build up others and put a smile on their faces or cut them down and leave them feeling hurt and depressed. "A tiny rudder makes a huge ship turn wherever the pilot wants it to go, even though the winds are strong. So also, the tongue is a small thing, but what enormous damage it can do" (James 3:4-5). Let's be the girl, the friend, whose words bring life.

There have been so many times when the cards and letters that I have received from people have changed my day. Some people take the time in their letters to offer words of encouragement and write down things they appreciate about me. They are just spreading a little cheer.

I keep those letters, and on days that seem dreary, I read them again. They serve to make me smile and give me hope.

Daily Step

*In order to increase your cheerfulness,
how about giving some away today?*

Day 68

The mouth of the righteous is a fountain of life, but violence overwhelms the mouth of the wicked.

PROVERBS 10:11, *NIV*

Our words have such power . . . perhaps more than we are aware of. I want the words that come out of my mouth to bring life to the person I am with or to whatever situation I am in. There is so much power in words of encouragement. People are drawn to those who encourage. So let's be great at it!

When you offer encouragement to someone, not only are you giving him or her a gift, but in that moment, by taking your eyes off of yourself, you are defeating self-centeredness. Sitting in the radiation waiting room put me in the company of many people who needed just a little encouragement. I have to admit that it was very easy to feel sorry for myself, but as I looked around the room, I saw many people who needed me to take my eyes off of myself and say something encouraging. My favorite sentence to say was, "One more day done!"

Most of us deal with fear and negativity from within and from without each day. We might even doubt whether we can finish whatever it is that we started out to do. There are so many times when an encouraging word is the difference between us quitting or continuing.

When Jesus entered a situation, He brought hope and encouragement. When people were freaking out and afraid, when they were at the end of their rope, His words brought encouragement. Ours should do the same.

Encouraging words are gifts. Make it a point to be encouraging to the people in your world. If you find it hard, you are just out of practice. Why do we find it easier to point out the weaknesses we see in someone rather than finding ways we can be her cheerleader? How can we so easily point out the area someone can improve in and find it hard to tell her where she is doing a great job? Develop the reputation of being the most encouraging person on the block!

Daily Step

Go on a criticism fast today . . . even if you have a legitimate criticism or even if you feel like your criticism is "constructive," don't share it. Just for today, let only encouraging words come out of your mouth.

Day 69

*This resurrection life you received from God
is not a timid, grave-tending life. It's adventurously
expectant, greeting God with a childlike
"What's next, Papa?"*

ROMANS 8:15, *THE MESSAGE*

I was walking through a cemetery in Wales with my family a number of years ago. We had found out that our ancestors had immigrated to the United States from Wales centuries ago. We discovered the town where most of them had lived, and we had fun exploring it.

In the cemetery, we found quite a few of their tombstones. It was interesting to see the dates . . . 1604-1655, 1783-1827. Yet while I was certainly curious about the dates my ancestors were born and died, I was more interested in the dash in between . . . because that tells me that they had lived.

What did they do with their dash? How did they live? What kind of work did they do? Did they love God? What did they do for fun?

There are going to be two dates written on your tombstone, too. I would like to suggest that the most important mark *is* that little dash. What are you doing with the life that you have been given?

If you were to win the lottery, or if you went on a game show and won thousands of dollars, what would you do with the money? Hide it under your bed? Probably not!

You would have serious fun spending it, or giving it away! And yet that money is nothing compared to what we have been given . . . abundant life. So let's not hide the life that we have been given under our bed!

We should be celebrating our life, not just trudging through the days, hanging on until Jesus comes! Jesus said that He came "so that everyone would have life, and have it in its fullest" (John 10:10, *CEV*). Christ wants us to lead full lives . . . He wants us to experience the joy that can be found in Him and get out there and share that joy with others. So, "don't be dejected and sad, for the joy of the Lord is your strength!" (Nehemiah 8:10, *NLT*).

If you take a look at the life that you have now and you are not crazy about it, make some changes. The life that you are now living is a result of seeds you sowed in days past, so if you want it to be different, sow new seeds rather than walking around resenting your life.

Daily Step

Sow some seeds today so that you will have the life you want tomorrow.

Day 70

This is how much God loved the world: He gave his Son, his one and only Son. And this is why: so that no one need be destroyed; by believing in him, anyone can have a whole and lasting life.

Dan was born with a degenerative heart condition. This problem was in remission for most of his childhood and teen years. He lived a normal kid's life filled with friends, baseball and drama. But in his junior year of high school, he had massive heart failure. By late 1980, he had spent several months at Sanford Medical Center, in what is called Life Row. He was waiting for a heart transplant. On December 22 the hospital sent Dan home for Christmas, expecting him to die before they could find a heart for him. But he was immediately rushed back to the hospital because they had a heart donor, and at age 17, Dan had a successful heart transplant operation.

Three days later on Christmas day, his mom read Luke 2 to Daniel while he was in recovery. Then she read the stacks of get-well cards from people all over the country who were praying for him. She pulled a card from the Midwest out of the pile and read the following note.[10]

Dear Dan,

Even though we do not know you, my husband and I feel so close to you and your family. Our only son, Lloyd, was your heart donor. Knowing that you have his heart has made our loss so much easier to bear.

—Paul and Barbara Chambers[11]

Dan wrote later about that experience:

I couldn't fight the tears any longer. And suddenly I knew more clearly than ever the real reason why I should be celebrating Christmas. In dying, the Chambers' only son had given me life. In dying, God's only son had given life, eternal life. Now I felt like shouting out loud my thanks that Jesus Christ was born!

"Thank you, Lord!" I said. "And bless you," I said as I thought of the young man who had signed the donor card that gave me my greatest Christmas present of all, "Bless you, Lloyd Chambers."[12]

God loved us so much that He gave His best. Jesus signed the donor card and said, "I will go. I will give My life on behalf of humanity . . . so that they can join Me in eternity."

Because of that great gift, how can we do any less than love?

Daily Step

*Read a few versions of John 3:16.
Get a clear picture of the gift you
have been given!*

And may [you] love the Lord your God, obey His voice, and cling to Him. For He is your life and the length of your days, that you may dwell in the land which the Lord swore to give to your fathers, to Abraham, Isaac, and Jacob.

DEUTERONOMY 30:20, *AMP* (EMPHASIS ADDED)

---

love *v:* a deep, tender, ineffable feeling of affection and solicitude toward a person, such as that arising from kinship, recognition of attractive qualities, or a sense of underlying oneness

You and I were created with a desire to love God. We were created with the ability to have a relationship with the Father . . . not a casual, every-now-and-then kind of relationship . . . but a passionate one!

When you were created . . . lovingly fashioned and formed . . . you were given a great gift: choice. You are not a puppet. While God longs for you to love Him, He can't and won't force you. As a bride, you weren't forced to love your husband, you chose to. Your husband's love for you wasn't compulsory; it was his choice. That is what makes love so powerful . . . it can't be forced . . . it is always freely given.

There is a scene in the movie *Bruce Almighty* in which the character that Jim Carey portrayed asked God (played by Morgan Freeman) how to make people love you. God answered, "When you figure that out, let me know." God desires our love and devotion. He created us to be His beloved Bride, and yet He can't force us to love Him. He just asks us to.

People have tried to make loving God mystical . . . but it isn't. Some people think that if they love God, they must take a vow of poverty, wear sackcloth and ashes, or walk over broken glass on their knees. *No!!* As if God would take pleasure in our pain!

So how do we let the Creator of the universe know that we love Him? Well, we can tell Him. Simply tell Him.

Another way that we communicate love is to spend time with the people we love. So take some time with your God. Read the Bible . . . His love letter to you. In the same way that you would anyone else you love, get to know who He is, what His likes and dislikes are, and what moves Him.

Love God . . . He loves you so much.

Daily Step

Tell God how much you love Him.
Lift your hands to heaven and just love
on your God for a few minutes.

Day 72

*Jesus replied: " 'Love the Lord your God with all your heart
and with all your soul and with all your mind.' This is the
first and greatest commandment. And the second is like it:
'Love your neighbor as yourself.' All the Law and the
Prophets hang on these two commandments."*

MATTHEW 22:37-40, *NIV*

---

pas·sion *n.* powerful, intense emotion, boundless enthusiasm

I have read novels over the years in which the husband and wife portrayed in the story are fairly indifferent to each other. They don't care what the other does as long as it doesn't interfere with their own lives. They don't hate each other . . . that would involve too much energy. They are simply bored and don't want to expend the energy needed to restore the relationship. They just live as disconnected roommates.

How sad. And it is sadder to realize that this scenario occurs not only in novels—there are some couples for whom this is a reality.

I love my husband . . . and not in a boring, bored, casual or apathetic way. While we certainly have quiet, pensive, relaxed moments, my love for Philip involves passion. Intense feeling.

My passion is evident when I see him after a few days of being apart from each other. My passion for him is evident when we have a disagreement. My passion is evident by how I listen to him. My passion is evident in the bedroom.

Passion . . . it is a good thing . . . and it keeps any relationship from being stuck in a rut.

When asked if they love God, some people reply, "Well, of course I love God. I go to church, don't I?" This is like saying that because you go home, you must love your husband. Jesus asked us to love God with *all* our heart, soul and mind.

Loving someone with all of your soul involves emotions. Loving someone with your entire mind involves intellect. We are not supposed to be passionless or brainless in our love for God. We are not to have an apathetic or casual love for our God.

Let's passionately love the Lover of our souls.

Daily Step

How can you passionately express your love for God?

Day 73

My beloved friends, let us continue to love each other since love comes from God. Everyone who loves is born of God and experiences a relationship with God. The person who refuses to love doesn't know the first thing about God, because God is love—so you can't know him if you don't love. This is how God showed his love for us: God sent his only Son into the world so we might live through him.

1 JOHN 4:7-9, *THE MESSAGE*

So many people in our world today have a hard time giving or receiving love. This is probably because they were not loved as children . . . and probably because they were not taught about the amazing love of their heavenly Father. If this is true in your life, I am sorry . . . and I am glad that you are on the journey toward love.

My children learned how to hug because Philip and I hugged them. They learned how to give kisses because we spent a lot of time kissing their cute faces! They learned to say "I love you" because they heard us saying it. They learned to love because they were loved.

The only reason I can love is because I am loved. God loved me so much that He sent His Son, His only Son, to Earth. He sent Jesus to pay the penalty for all my failures. Jesus died so that I could live. Is there any greater love than that? I don't think so.

Jesus came so that I could have a relationship with God. His sacrifice "cleared away my sin and the damage it did to my relationship with God." Jesus stepped out of heaven and came to Earth to pay for sins He didn't commit. He did it because He loved. As His little sister, I don't think I am to do any less. I am to spend my life loving humanity. So are you.

One of the greatest ways to communicate my love for God is to love you. Since I am loved so greatly, I can now love others. So can you. We show God that we love Him by how we love each other.

Jesus told us that the world would know we are His disciples . . . not by the big Bible we carry, not by the clever bumper sticker on our car, not by how many times we go to church . . . but by our love for one another. We must get great at loving each other. In spite of different backgrounds, different personality styles, different cultures, different tastes . . . we must become experts at love.

Daily Step

Is there anyone you can think of who is the epitome of love? What is one practical way that you can "love your neighbor as yourself"?

This is the kind of love we are talking about—not that we once upon a time loved God, but that he loved us and sent his Son as a sacrifice to clear away our sins and the damage they've done to our relationship with God.

1 JOHN 4:10, *THE MESSAGE*

Day 74

Go after a life of love as if your life depended on it—
because it does. Give yourselves to the gifts God gives you.
Most of all, try to proclaim his truth.

1 CORINTHIANS 14:1

Sometimes it is much easier to love from afar then to love those who live in my house! My husband is a wonderful man, however there are times when loving him is *hard!* I always think, *If only he were more like me!* Because, after all, I am practically perfect (ha!), and so if he was like me, it would be much easier.

My job is to love anyway . . . and to get great at communicating love to my husband. If you are married, ask your husband what makes him feel loved (and I guarantee you it is more than just sex!).

Philip likes to watch baseball . . . live and on TV. I am not crazy about sitting in front of the television. I didn't grow up watching it, so it just isn't fun for me. But because I love my husband and want to demonstrate that love . . . I sit with him and watch those Yankees go for it!

You and I are great multitaskers, but most men aren't. They are not wrong, just different. You and I could be having a conversation, cooking dinner and helping our child with homework all at the same time. Neither one of us would feel that the other is not listening.

Most men are not that way. If we are not giving them 100 percent of our visual attention, they feel like we are not listening . . . even if we can repeat back what they just said. My husband is like this, so I have learned to stop doing those other things when he needs me to listen to him. Why? Because I want to communicate that he is important to me and that I love him.

com·mu·ni·ca·tion *n:* the exchange of thoughts, messages or information, as by speech, signals, writing or behavior

Communication involves more than just the words we say to our husbands. It involves demonstrating through our words *and* actions that we are listening to them. It means putting our interests aside so that we can become actively involved in our husbands' lives . . . even when we don't feel like it.

So let's become experts . . . or at least close to it . . . at loving our husbands. Let's pursue a life of love as if our lives depended on it. Let's become experts at actually communicating love so that our husbands feel it. How amazing would our world be if every husband and wife truly demonstrated such love to each other?

Daily Step

Go buy a book on marriage or relationships—and then read it!

Day 75

This is what I command you: that you love one another.

JOHN 15:17, *AMP*

It is so easy to become overwhelmed by the tragedy that we see happening every single day all over the earth. We cannot ignore it and we cannot turn our heads from the pain we see in humanity. Instead, we have to get great at loving . . . one person at a time. It starts in your home—with your husband and your family, and then with your friends and the single parent in your life . . . one person at a time.

Sometimes, as we examine the suffering around us, we can feel powerless to change it. The truth is that there are many opportunities for you and me to reach hurting people. I would bet that you would not have to drive farther than your own street. Plato said, "Be kind, for everyone is fighting a harder battle." Humans are humans no matter where you go, and you never know what people are actually dealing with at home.

"You are a garden fountain, a well of living water, as refreshing as the streams from the Lebanon mountains" (Song of Songs 4:15, *NLT*). God calls you a "garden fountain." You are a well of living water. You are refreshing. I love that picture! Isn't it great to know that you are a refreshing breath of air on this planet?

There may be a woman with HIV who needs you to refresh her thoughts on life . . . on love . . . on God. There may be a woman struggling in her marriage—I bet you have a few answers to her questions. There are very simple ways to love people: prepare someone a meal, treat a family to lunch, drive an older woman to church, focus on loving your husband instead of thinking of the ways he should be loving you.

You have something to give, and if our living God lives in your heart, there is enough love inside you for humanity . . . for the broken . . . for the discarded . . . for the unwanted and forgotten . . . for the unlovable.

My friend Shanelle says this: "Jesus' message of love and hope was a global one, but He lived it out locally." Remember: One person at a time. Start where you are with the people in your corner of the world. It is incredible to have the chance to travel the globe and offer hope, but sometimes it takes greater strength to knock on your neighbor's door and offer *her* hope.

Daily Step

What is one practical thing that you can do today to demonstrate love for someone in your world? Do it.

*To you who are ready for the truth, I say this:
Love your enemies. Let them bring out the best
in you, not the worst. When someone gives you
a hard time, respond with the energies
of prayer for that person.*

LUKE 6:27-28, *THE MESSAGE*

I was sitting near the front on one of those smaller airplanes waiting for takeoff. I actually had an empty seat next to me, which I was happy about because now I could stretch out another three inches . . . yippee! Just then, a woman boarded the plane and began complaining. She was not happy about the size of the aircraft or the fact that her carry-on would not fit in the overhead compartment. She complained about the delay in takeoff and just about everything else.

Much to my chagrin, this angry woman was seated next to me. Not only did I lose my precious three inches, but now I also had grouchy woman sitting next to me. Sigh.

I opened a book, turned away from the woman and began to read. But I hadn't even finished one page when I heard a voice from heaven whisper, "Ask her how she is doing." *What*?! God wanted me to talk to this mean woman?? I don't think so! So, I just sat there, pretending to read.

A few minutes went by, and I knew that I needed to obey the voice of my Father. So, with great trepidation, I asked the woman how she was doing. She turned and looked and me and then started crying. She said that she had just found out that she had a fatal disease and was headed home to talk to doctors. I began to talk to her, pat her hand, pray for her and offer help in whatever way I could.

What if I had ignored the whisper of my God? What if I had let my prejudice against an angry woman keep me from opening my mouth?

On a hot day, Jesus sat down at a well to rest. It was no accident that Jesus picked this well, on this day, at this time. This was about to be a divine appointment. He asked a Samaritan woman at the well if she would get Him a drink of water. She was stunned that He spoke to her. She was a Samaritan, a woman and a sinner . . . and yet Jesus spoke to her. He wasn't judging her condition, although He was aware of it. He accepted her. Just by speaking to her, He gave her value. His acceptance and love opened her heart so that soon after, she ran to the town to tell the people all about this man called Jesus.

Let's make sure we are known more for our love and acceptance than judgment.

Daily Step

Read the story of the woman at the well in John 4. What does this story say to you?

Day 77

> *Jesus said, "Father, forgive these people, because they*
> *don't know what they are doing." And the soldiers*
> *gambled for his clothes by throwing dice.*
>
> LUKE 23:34, *NLT*

At some point during the Korean War, the communists arrested a South Korean Christian civilian and ordered him to be killed. However, a young communist leader discovered that the civilian was the director of an orphanage that cared for small children. He decided to spare the man's life; so, instead he ordered the man's son be shot in his place. So they shot the man's 19-year-old son, right in front of him.

Afterward, the positions of war changed and UN forces captured the young communist leader. He stood trial and was sentenced to death. Amazingly, before the punishment could be carried out, the Christian civilian came to beg for the young leader's life . . . the very same man who had murdered his son. The civilian explained that the young leader really did not realize what he had done and asked the court to give the young man to him, saying, "Give him to me and I will train him."

The UN forces approved the civilian's request, and he took the former communist leader and cared for him—in his own home. The great love and restoration that this father provided for the young communist opened the young man's eyes to the love of Christ. Today, the same young man who had once been a murderer is now a Christian pastor, following and serving Jesus.[13]

I am always so touched by . . . and a little in awe of . . . this kind of forgiveness. I get bothered when someone lies about me or says something mean! Recently, I had to sit in silence as someone began saying horrible things about me. I couldn't defend myself or retaliate. It was one of the hardest things I have had to do. Or at least I thought it was . . . until I got home and realized that I had to forgive that person.

One of my jobs is to demonstrate to the best of my ability the love of Jesus to the people in my world. And that involves forgiving. Forgiving is never easy. Wanting vengeance is easier. But if Jesus forgave His murderers, I am called to do no less . . . and neither are you.

Daily Step

Who in your world do you need to forgive? Begin forgiving. It starts with a decision of your will . . . and you might have to forgive a few times until it moves to your heart.

Day 78

So this is my prayer: that your love will flourish and that you will not only love much but well. Learn to love appropriately. You need to use your head and test your feelings so that your love is sincere and intelligent, not sentimental gush. Live a lover's life, circumspect and exemplary, a life Jesus will be proud of: bountiful in fruits from the soul, making Jesus Christ attractive to all, getting everyone involved in the glory and praise of God.

PHILIPPIANS 1:9-10, *THE MESSAGE*

---

flour·ish *v:* to grow well or luxuriantly; thrive

I must confess . . . I love a good romance. I like a book or a movie that has a love story in it. And my husband, who knows this about me, will say, "Holly, let's go see this movie . . . it has a relationship in it and everything." (It probably also has a few explosions, but according to him, there is at least one relationship!)

While it is okay to like a romance, don't make the mistake of thinking that real love is like a romance book or movie. Real love is not about perfect lighting that makes our skin look great, or perfect clothes, or perfect people. Real love is about real people making a real effort to love other real people.

Our love should be "sincere and intelligent, not sentimental gush." Love isn't just about what we feel . . . real love involves doing. God loved us so much that He did something . . . He gave His Son. As lovers on the earth, our love should be real, practical and fruitful. The love we express should make "Jesus Christ attractive to all."

Are you loving people in a way that draws them to Jesus? I have had a number of people over the years tell me that what drew them to church was the love they saw between the people there . . . not gushy, sentimental love, but love that was sincere. Most people are thirsty for love and acceptance. They can get it from Jesus . . . but oftentimes they need to see it in us first.

The dictionary states that the word "love" can be a noun. But more important, the word "love" can also be a verb. Love is the action we take; the expression we make that brings a little heaven to Earth. It is our job to not only experience the love of our Father but also to be His hand and demonstrate that love on a daily basis to those we meet.

Daily Step

What are three practical ways that you can demonstrate love today? Do them.

Day 79

Greater love has no one than this, that he lay down his life for his friends.

JOHN 15:13, *NIV*

A man named Sadhu Sundar Singh was once traveling with a companion high in the Himalayan Mountains when they stumbled across a body lying in the snow. Sundar Singh wanted to stop and help the man, who would certainly die without their help, but his friend refused to stop, crying, "We shall lose our lives if we burden ourselves with him."

Sundar Singh could not bring himself to leave the man to die. His companion said goodbye and went on ahead. Sundar Singh utilized all his strength to lift the man onto his back and carry him forward. Although it was a strain on his body, the heat from Sundar Singh's body began to warm the frozen man, and eventually the man was rejuvenated. Before long, they were able to begin walking side by side. As they made their journey together to catch up with Sundar Singh's former companion, they soon found him—lying dead in the snow . . . frozen by the cold.[14]

I am not sure how many times you may be called on to give your actual life for someone. But I do know that you will be asked to lay down your rights . . . even what is convenient . . .

for someone else. I don't know about you, but for me there are times when taking a bullet for someone might be easier than laying down my ego!

Sometimes when I am having an intense discussion (argument) with Philip, I will just stop trying to make my point known. Any argument takes at least two people to keep it going. Generally, I like to have the last word . . . I like to prove my point . . . but because I love my husband, sometimes I just stop trying to prove anything. I lay down my ego. And I have to tell you, it is not easy . . . at least not for me.

There are times when I am asked to go out of my way to do something for someone. And honestly, my first thought is, *How can I get out of this?* Thank God we don't have to give in to our first thought! My second thought is usually to find a way to do it, because love, real love, will mean inconveniencing myself sometimes.

Daily Step

Instead of trying to prove your point to someone today, just be quiet and listen to him or her. And do something for someone that is inconvenient for you.

Day 80

Love never gives up . . . Love doesn't want what it doesn't have. Love doesn't strut, Doesn't have a swelled head, Doesn't force itself on others, Isn't always "me first," Doesn't fly off the handle, Doesn't keep score of the sins of others, Doesn't revel when others grovel, Takes pleasure in the flowering of truth, Puts up with anything, Trusts God always, Always looks for the best, Never looks back, But keeps going to the end.

1 CORINTHIANS 13:4-7,13, *THE MESSAGE*

"Love extravagantly" . . . well, there's a goal! Love might be mysterious in how it springs up, but it is very practical in how it is lived out. Love doesn't just exist out there in the cosmos . . . love has to be directed somewhere.

In these verses, Paul is giving the Corinthian church some very practical advice on how to love. He starts out by saying that love doesn't give up. Good advice, because there are going to be moments on this journey of love when it will get hard and you will want to quit demonstrating love.

Real love then asks the question, What would be good for _____?—not what would be good for me. If we all did this, I wonder how many fewer lawsuits there would be?

Real love says, "You go first . . . you have first pick." Real love is not like the seagulls in *Finding Nemo*, who kept squawking "Mine!" when they saw a tasty fish! Real love says, "Go ahead!"

Real love doesn't hold the mistakes of the past against you. A counselor once told me about a couple that came into his office. The wife said that she had had it with her husband's black book. The counselor, thinking that he understood what the black book was, told the woman, "I can understand why."

But the counselor was even more shocked when the woman revealed that inside of this black book, her husband kept a record of everything she had done wrong in their marriage since it began! In his mind, the husband was using the black book to "help" her. How sad that he did not understand that real love doesn't keep score of wrongdoings. Real love forgives.

Daily Step

First Peter 4:8 says, "Above all things have fervent love for one another, for 'love will cover a multitude of sins'" (NKJV). What does this verse say to you?

Day 81

*No, we neither make nor save ourselves. God does both the
making and saving. He creates each of us by Christ Jesus to
join him in the work he does, the good work he has gotten
ready for us to do, work we had better be doing.*

EPHESIANS 2:10, *THE MESSAGE*

*My dear friends, stand firm and don't be shaken.
Always keep busy working for the Lord. You know that
everything you do for him is worthwhile.*

1 CORINTHIANS 15:58, *CEV*

The alarm goes off in the morning and the work of the day
begins. Grab a shot of wheatgrass (yuck) . . . spend quiet time
with my God . . . work out . . . make breakfast for the family . . .
make lunches . . . shower . . . go off to work . . . attend meetings .
. . write . . . make phone calls . . . train . . . create . . . think . . . study
. . . prepare for a trip . . . go to Paris's basketball game . . . what's
for dinner? . . . help with homework . . . have family time . . . husband time . . . read . . . good night . . .

And then it all starts again!

I do lead a busy and full life. There were times when I felt
that perhaps I needed to apologize for it . . . but no longer. Busy
is not bad. The apostle Paul was busy; Jesus was busy. I am busy

"working for the Lord." My day is spent in moments strung together. Each moment is one in which I am pursuing, to the best of my ability, the purpose for which I was created.

I have found that my teenagers get into trouble when they have too much idle time. Rest time is good. Idle time is not. We were created for action.

Now, maybe you are busy pursuing things that you shouldn't be. Maybe you are wasting time investing in areas in which you don't belong—not necessarily bad areas, just areas that are not part of the path that God has designed for you. It is being busy pursuing things that don't matter . . . things that don't produce good fruit . . . things that are not pleasing to God . . . things that don't build His kingdom . . . that are the problem.

You were created to join your God in the work He does. You were not created to sit around and watch, but rather to be an active participant in seeing the work of God fulfilled on the earth. He had great plans for you when He breathed life into you. You have been recreated in Christ so that you can fulfill all that God had in mind for you. He has gotten you ready to do good work. I can't do your part. No one else can.

You and I should be leading a full life. You only get one. Make this one count.

Daily Step

Take a real look at your day.
Are you busy pursuing the things of God,
or are you just busy?

Day 82

So—join the company of good men and women,
keep your feet on the tried and true paths. It's the men
who walk straight who will settle this land, the women
with integrity who will last here.

Proverbs 2:20-21, *The Message*

---

last *v:* to persist or endure for the entire length of

It is comforting to me to know that I am a part of something bigger. My part is very important, but it is not the whole (which takes the pressure off!).

Recently, our church raised money to send to an organization called "Smile Train." This organization trains local doctors in various countries around the world to repair the faces of children who suffer from cleft palate. Our church sent over $24,000, which would help put smiles on the faces of about 94 children! How awesome is that?!

I will be forever grateful that I am a part of an incredible company of men and women who partner together in making a difference in our world. You are too. You are a part of a company . . . a great company of men and women all over the world. And with each of us doing our part, we will "settle this land."

We will bring a little of heaven to Earth.

This last month, I have watched my daughter play a lot of basketball games. During the first game, I noticed that before the game had even progressed into the second half, my daughter was out of breath. And while she played her best during the second half, it wasn't quite up to her performance in the first half. I was wondering if she would last. However, now, after many hours of practice and conditioning, sometimes her best performance occurs in the last quarter. She has trained herself into a player that lasts.

You need to be a woman who lasts. Maybe you feel a little weak and out of shape now, but you can condition yourself into a woman who is as strong at the end of the day as you were at the beginning. It just takes practice and commitment to endure.

Be the woman who doesn't bail out at her job. Be the woman who lasts in her marriage. Be the woman who lasts in her church. Be the woman who lasts in her friendships.

Daily Step

One of the definitions of "integrity" is "the quality or condition of being whole or undivided." Does that describe you? If not, are you committed to the journey of wholeness?

Day 83

*Blessed are those whose strength is in you, who have
set their hearts on pilgrimage.*

PSALM 84:5, *NIV*

---

pil·grim·age *n:* a long journey or search, especially one
of exalted purpose or moral significance

In between my junior and senior year of High School, my family and I took a long trip in an RV. We drove from Texas all the way up through New England so that I could interview at about 13 different universities (hadn't quite made up my mind yet!). No one in our family had ever been in an RV. We were not the camping family—I am not sure what we would have done if we had been left on a deserted island (frightening thought). Our idea of "roughing it" was staying in a hotel with no room service, so I have no idea what we were thinking when we began this great RV adventure! We had some very funny moments though. At least funny for me!

The RV broke down before we even got out of Texas, so we spent hours at the mechanics while it was being repaired. We then arrived at the RV park so late that night that we couldn't see to hook up any of our hoses. A night without a toilet . . .

joy. We were in such tight quarters that we all heard every sound that each of us made . . . every sound . . . joy.

On one particular day my dad was tired of driving, so he pulled over to let my mom take over. While we were stopped, he began to climb the short ladder behind the driver's seat so that he could rest in the bed that was there. Well, my mom did not wait for him to get settled—she was on a mission. She took off . . . and so did my dad. He flew through the air from the front of the RV to the back and landed on the table, shouting, "Sherrrrryyyyyy!" all the way. I laughed until tears were streaming down my cheeks. I think it took him a few years to think it was funny!

Our long journey, our pilgrimage, did finally come to an end, and I did get accepted into the college of my choice. So at least those weeks in a crowded RV paid off!

It is good to have adventures and travel to new places, but it is even more important to keep our minds on the move . . . to try new things and think new thoughts. And it is even better to keep our hearts committed to the long journey of walking out our purpose.

Don't get stuck doing the same old thing. War against being average.

Daily Step

Try something new today.

He sent back this answer: "Do not think that because you are in the king's house you alone of all the Jews will escape. For if you remain silent at this time, relief and deliverance for the Jews will arise from another place, but you and your father's family will perish. And who knows but that you have come to royal position for such a time as this?"

ESTHER 4:13-14, *NIV*

King Solomon said that everything had a season and a time (see Ecclesiastes 3:1). So that means there is a time to speak up and a time to be silent. The tricky part is learning which is which.

There have been times when I spoke up and just created more chaos. And there have been times that I was silent when it would have served God better for me to speak up.

Esther faced a moment like that. She had won the beauty pageant and was enjoying life in the palace. When she heard that Haman was plotting to kill the Jews, she felt bad, but didn't know what she could do. But her cousin Mordecai reminded her that perhaps God had made her royalty in order to do good . . . and to do it right now.

The Hebrew word for "Esther" is *Hadassah*, which means "myrtle." The myrtle bush is a beautiful and fragrant one. It can also stand up to any kind of weather.

The same was true of Esther. She was certainly beautiful, and in the midst of a threat she rose to the challenge. She risked her life and went to plead her case before the king. He heard her, believed her, and helped her.

So on an ordinary day, an orphaned girl with a past was used by God to save His people.

You and I have risen to a position of royalty so that we can speak up for those unable to speak for themselves. We have risen to the position of royalty so that we can go about doing good.

Edmond Burke said, "All that is necessary for the triumph of evil is that good men do nothing." In our time, let's be the people who do whatever it takes for the goodness of God to prevail. Let's not remain silent when speaking up would help.

Daily Step

Can you think of a time when you should have spoken up . . . when you should have risked something . . . but didn't? Make a decision that this won't be the case again!

Day 85

Upon entering, Gabriel greeted her: "Good morning! You're beautiful with God's beauty, Beautiful inside and out! God be with you."

LUKE 1:28, *THE MESSAGE*

My husband is a pretty wonderful man, but I don't think I can remember a time when the first words out of his mouth to me were, "Good morning, Holly, you are beautiful inside and out!" I usually just get a mumble from him on his way to the coffee pot. Well, the truth is . . . I have never started my day with "Good morning, Philip, you are one good-looking man!" Maybe I should start . . . I think I will . . . tomorrow. Won't he be shocked?!

Whether or not anyone in your family tells you how beautiful you are first thing in the morning . . . your heavenly Father will. He wants you to begin your day knowing how lovely He thinks you are. When I choose to spend time with God each morning, I sense His love and feel His joy. As I read His Word, He tells me that I am beautiful. And He is not talking about the condition of my hair or my lack of makeup. He is focused on my heart and my soul.

We spend hours working on our outside . . . and there is nothing wrong with making the most of what we have. After all, there are a lot of people looking at your outside—might as well give them something pretty to look at! ☺

There is nothing wrong with trying new styles or wanting to look your prettiest. Go ahead; give it all you've got! But the sad truth is that age happens to us all . . . and the one thing that is sure to change is your looks. So, in all of your beautifying, make sure you are beautifying your heart.

I have met some elderly women who are bitter and angry at the life they have. In looking at their old photos, I could see beautiful young women. But unfortunately, they spent more time on their hair and makeup then they did on their soul, because now, in the sunset of their life . . . they are not so pretty on the inside.

You beautify your heart and soul when you live a life that is surrendered to your God. Your heart is beautiful when you say yes to your God . . . when you allow Him to mold you, correct you and cleanse you.

Daily Step

*Listen and hear the Lover of your soul
tell you how beautiful you are!*

Day 86

The night is about over, dawn is about to break.
Be up and awake to what God is doing! God is putting
the finishing touches on the salvation work he began
when we first believed.

ROMANS 13:12, *THE MESSAGE*

I have some friends who are amazing. They can fall fast asleep during any movie. I don't mean the two-minute quiet catnap— I mean the snoring, head-rolling kind of sleep. It doesn't matter if it is a love story or a movie filled with lots of car chases and explosions; they fall asleep. They just paid $9 for a two-hour nap. I don't get it. I tell them, "Look, if you are so tired, you can take a nap and we can see the movie later." They tell me that it doesn't matter. Regardless of when they see the movie, they would sleep. OK . . . whatever. Still don't get it.

While I think it is fairly pathetic to fall asleep in a movie, it is even worse to sleep through life. In this verse, the apostle Paul is telling the Romans (and us) to wake up!

Turn on any news channel for even a minute and you will hear about some pain or suffering somewhere in the world. You will hear about a virus that is frightening people. You will hear about another natural disaster that has cost thousands of lives and millions of dollars in damage. You might hear of someone who has been murdered or abducted. Yes, there are tragic happenings going on in our world. We need to be awake to them so that we can help. We can pray, we can offer financial help where needed, and we can lead the fearful to a relationship with their Creator.

At the same time, we need to be awake to what God is doing. There are great things happening all over the earth. Recently, I saw a video of a man preaching in Africa, and there were more than one million people in the audience. There was an endless sea of people making a decision to follow God. In China, millions of believers gather in secret meetings. Hundreds of them sacrifice their lives for what they believe. In South America, thousands of young people gather . . . not to cause trouble, but to worship God.

All over the earth, God is moving on the hearts of men and women. He is "putting the finishing touches on the salvation work He began." He is gathering His Bride.

Wake up and see the glory of our God!

Daily Step

Thank God for what He is doing around the earth! Ask Him what you can do to alleviate someone else's pain and fear. This could be someone in your sphere . . . it doesn't have to be someone way around the globe.

Day 87

We are assured and know that [God being a partner in their labor] all things work together and are [fitting into a plan] for good to and for those who love God and are called according to [His] design and purpose.

ROMANS 8:28, *AMP*

I am not very good at crafts that involve yarn, needles or thread (but give me a glue gun and watch out!). My mom, on the other hand, has done some amazing things with just a needle and thread. She creates true works of art. One thing, however, that I have noticed in all of these projects involving thread is that the back of the project doesn't look like a work of art . . . it looks like a tangled mess of threads.

Ephesians 2:10 says that you are God's work of art . . . His masterpiece. You may not always feel like a work of art, but you are. You are a tapestry that God is creating. The only thing is . . . God works from the backside of the tapestry. He takes all the tangled threads of our life and forms us into His masterpiece.

If you let Him in, He will use all the threads of your life . . . those that come from bad choices, those that come just from time and chance, those that come from the enemy, and those He brings. He will take all these threads and create something beautiful, because "all things work together for good" for those of us who love God.

I know it can be hard to believe, because we see our flaws . . . we see the mistakes . . . we see the pain.

We might not like the color of the thread. Maybe there is a tangled black thread on the back of your tapestry. Maybe it is the thread that came when your husband left you . . . or when you got a very bad report from a doctor. Of course you are hurt and angry, but if you let God in, He will make all things work together for good.

You might ask, "How?"

I don't know . . . I don't know how He put the stars in the sky; I just know that He did . . . I don't know how my car works; I just know it does.

But I do know that *all* things work together for good to those who love Him. Surrendered to Him, all things can be used in the masterpiece.

Daily Step

Make a decision to trust your Father today that all things . . . good or bad . . . can be worked for your good.

Day 88

Let us not become weary in doing good, for at the proper time we will reap a harvest if we do not give up. Therefore, as we have opportunity, let us do good to all people, especially to those who belong to the family of believers

GALATIANS 6:9-10, *NIV*

I love watching my kids play basketball. And the truth is, I do more than watch . . . I am very vocally involved! There have been games in which my daughter's team excelled in defense. The opposing team hardly made any shots. But in order to win games, a good defense is not enough.

At some point, offense must take over. I love it when my daughter is so tough on defense that she steals the ball from her opponent and then races to our basket to lay in two points. She started out in a position of defense and ended up on offense.

As you and I navigate the journey of life, we must be great at both defense and offense. Right now I am on the offense against a disease that is trying to take me out. I started out on the defense . . . just trying to remain standing when I got the diagnosis. But I soon realized that I had to move into an offensive position if I was going to beat the cancer.

I am frying (radiation treatments) any remaining cancer cells, and I have changed my diet to one that strengthens my immune system. When our immune systems are strong, it makes it hard for disease to live. Offense and defense.

In any relationship, we are always on both offense and defense, doing things that would prevent problems and attacking any problems until victory is accomplished.

It sounds exhausting.

It can be.

We were given a sword and a shield to fight the good fight. In order to win, we need to be proficient at both.

Just don't "grow weary in doing good," because you will receive the harvest you want if you keep on. Keep raising your shield and swinging your sword.

Daily Step

In your life today, where are you on offense? Defense? Do you need to be better at raising your shield or swinging your sword?

{ Day 89 }

*For you have need of steadfast patience and endurance,
so that you may perform and fully accomplish the will of
God, and thus receive and carry away [and enjoy
to the full] what is promised.*

Hebrews 10:36, *AMP*

---

en·dur·ance *n:* the act, quality, or power of withstanding
hardship or stress

Philip and I love to scuba dive. There is something magical about
being in the ocean. The colors of the fish and coral amaze me.
How creative is our God! He didn't miss a trick!

There are some very important things we learned in our scuba
certification class. When we were on the beach, the air around us
had a pressure of 14.7 PSI (pounds per square inch), or 1 atmo-
sphere. When you scuba dive, you must breathe from a scuba tank.

The air coming out of the tank has the same pressure as the
pressure that the water is exerting. It must, or it wouldn't come
out of the tank. So, when we were diving, the air in our lungs at a
depth of 33 feet has twice the pressure of air on land, and the air
in our lungs at a depth of 66 feet has three times the pressure.

So the pressure on the inside has to match the pressure on
the outside. Think of a submarine . . . it has to be pressurized

so that it can withstand great depths, otherwise it would collapse.

pres·sure *n:* Urgent claim or demand; an oppressive condition of physical, mental, social, or economic distress.

You and I must get great at handling pressure. Every day brings with it its own levels of stress. We just need a greater "pressure" on the inside of us so that we don't collapse.

By having a real relationship with our God and by determining that we will accomplish what He put us on the earth to do, we build up the pressure on the inside so that when pressure comes at us on the outside, we don't collapse. We have a long life to live. We can't wilt with every hardship that comes along.

Make a decision to be someone who endures.

Don't be a quitter.

Don't let the pressures of life cause you to collapse.

Daily Step

Read Hebrews 6:12. What does this verse say to you?

Day 90

God is the one who began this good work in you,
and I am certain that he won't stop before it is complete
on the day that Christ Jesus returns.

PHILIPPIANS 1:6, CEV

You have surrendered your heart to your God.

You are spending time every day with Him.

You have asked Him for help in growing up . . . in maturing.

You are becoming more and more comfortable with the crown on your head.

You have surrounded yourself with great people.

You are extending your hand to those who need help.

You are opening your heart and loving those whom God brings across your path.

You are forgiving those who hurt you.

You are learning to put your armor on . . . and you are comfortable with your sword.

You are ready and willing to go to war against the enemy when necessary.

You will never give up.

You are a continual learner.

You smile, even when it is hard.

You are a GodChick!

You are amazing.

Final Step

Go ahead and pat yourself on the
back . . . you have finished this book!
Now, go get another one!

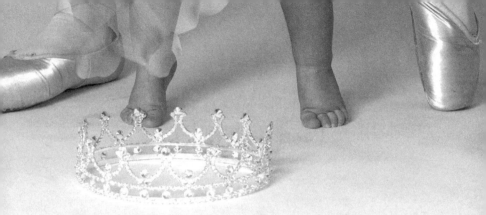

Taking the First Step . . .

Maybe you have never begun your own adventure with Jesus. Maybe you don't have a real relationship with your Creator. Maybe you believe in some kind of higher power . . . but I don't think that is going to help you in your daily life. You were created to have a real, powerful and life-changing relationship with God.

God sent Jesus to the earth to pay the price for your weaknesses and failings. He did it because He loves you so much and wants to have a relationship with you. He created eternity with you in mind. He wants to be with you forever, but the only way that can happen is if you accept His gift—His gift of Jesus.

So right now, open your heart to the greatest love you will ever know! Open your heart to the greatest gift ever given . . . realize that you are loved. Just the way you are. Pray this prayer . . . and make it yours.

Father, thank You for loving me so much that You sent Jesus to pay a debt I could never pay. Today, I choose You. Today, I accept Your love. Thank You for Your forgiveness. I thank You that from this moment on, I am a new person . . . from this moment on, I am a follower of Jesus Christ.

God's Word for GodChicks®

Healing

Heal me, O LORD, and I will be healed; save me and I will be saved, for you are the one I praise.
Jeremiah 17:14-15, *NIV*

Jesus turned and saw her. "Take heart, daughter," he said, "your faith has healed you." And the woman was healed from that moment.
Matthew 9:21-23, *NIV*

Nevertheless, I will bring health and healing to it; I will heal my people and will let them enjoy abundant peace and security.
Jeremiah 33:6, *NIV*

Is it not to share your food with the hungry and to provide the poor wanderer with shelter-when you see the naked, to clothe him, and not to turn away from your own flesh and blood? Then your light will break forth like the dawn, and your healing will quickly appear; then your righteousness will go before you, and the glory of the LORD will be your rear guard. Then you will call, and the LORD will answer; you will cry for help, and he will say: Here am I.
Isaiah 58:7-9, *NIV*

But for you who fear my name, the Sun of Righteousness will rise with healing in his wings. And you will go free, leaping with joy like calves let out to pasture.
Malachi 4:2, *NLT*

They had come to hear him and to be healed, and Jesus cast out many evil spirits. Everyone was trying to touch him, because healing power went out from him, and they were all cured.
Luke 6:18-19, NLT

The name of Jesus has healed this man-and you know how lame he was before. Faith in Jesus' name has caused this healing before your very eyes.
Acts 3:16, NLT

Then they were on the road. They preached with joyful urgency that life can be radically different; right and left they sent the demons packing; they brought wellness to the sick, anointing their bodies, healing their spirits.
Mark 6:12-13, THE MESSAGE

Peace

I'm leaving you well and whole. That's my parting gift to you. Peace. I don't leave you the way you're used to being left-feeling abandoned, bereft. So don't be upset. Don't be distraught.
John 14:27, THE MESSAGE

But now, O Israel, the LORD who created you says: "Do not be afraid, for I have ransomed you. I have called you by name; you are mine. When you go through deep waters and great trouble, I will be with you. When you go through rivers of difficulty, you will not drown! When you walk through the fire of oppression, you will not be burned up; the flames will not consume you.
Isaiah 43:1-2, NLT

"For I know the plans I have for you," says the LORD. "They are plans for good and not for disaster, to give you a future and a hope."
Jeremiah 29:11, NLT

Don't fret or worry. Instead of worrying, pray. Let petitions and praises shape your worries into prayers, letting God know your concerns. Before

you know it, a sense of God's wholeness, everything coming together for good, will come and settle you down. It's wonderful what happens when Christ displaces worry at the center of your life.
Philippians 4:6-7, THE MESSAGE

God is our refuge and strength, an ever-present help in trouble. Therefore we will not fear, though the earth give way and the mountains fall into the heart of the sea, though its waters roar and foam and the mountains quake with their surging.
Psalm 46:1-3, NIV

For God has not given us a spirit of fear, but of power and of love and of a sound mind.
2 Timothy 1:7, NKJV

There is no fear in love; but perfect love casts out fear, because fear involves torment.
1 John 4:18, NKJV

There is no fear in love [dread does not exist], but full-grown (complete, perfect) love turns fear out of doors and expels every trace of terror! For fear brings with it the thought of punishment, and [so] he who is afraid has not reached the full maturity of love [is not yet grown into love's complete perfection].
1 John 4:18, AMP

Strength

But those who hope in the LORD will renew their strength. They will soar on wings like eagles; they will run and not grow weary, they will walk and not be faint.
Isaiah 40:31, NIV

But I will sing of your strength, in the morning I will sing of your love; for you are my fortress, my refuge in times of trouble. O my Strength, I sing praise to you; you, O God, are my fortress, my loving God.
Psalm 59:16-18, *NIV*

I pulled you in from all over the world, called you in from every dark corner of the earth, telling you, "You're my servant, serving on my side. I've picked you. I haven't dropped you.' Don't panic. I'm with you. There's no need to fear for I'm your God. I'll give you strength. I'll help you. I'll hold you steady, keep a firm grip on you."
Isaiah 41:9-11, *THE MESSAGE*

I'm singing joyful praise to GOD. I'm turning cartwheels of joy to my Savior God. Counting on GOD's Rule to prevail, I take heart and gain strength. I run like a deer. I feel like I'm king of the mountain!
Habakkuk 3:18-19, *THE MESSAGE*

She is clothed with strength and dignity; she can laugh at the days to come.
Proverbs 31:25, *NIV*

I know how to be abased, and I know how to abound. Everywhere and in all things I have learned both to be full and to be hungry, both to abound and to suffer need. I can do all things through Christ who strengthens me.
Philippians 4:12-13, *NKJV*

Daily Steps Bible Reading Plan

Below is a daily Bible reading plan that will help you as you continue to take steps each day in your walk with God. Each day's readings consist of two parts: a general reading and a "devotion" taken from the books of poetry and the psalms. Note that not all of the books of the Bible have been included in this one-year plan . . . to make your reading a bit easier, chapters of the Bible containing detailed accounts of the Law of Moses (such as Leviticus), long genealogical tables and lists (as in Numbers) and repetitions of Jewish history (such as 1 and 2 Chronicles) have been omitted.

Date	Reading	Devotion
☐ January 1	Genesis 1—2	Job 1—2
☐ January 2	Genesis 3—4	Job 3
☐ January 3	Genesis 5—6	
☐ January 4	Genesis 7—8	Job 4
☐ January 5	Genesis 9—11	
☑ January 6	Genesis 12—13	Job 5
☐ January 7	Genesis 14—15	
☐ January 8	Genesis 16—17	Job 6
☐ January 9	Genesis 18—19	
☐ January 10	Genesis 20—22	Job 7
☐ January 11	Genesis 23—24	
☐ January 12	Genesis 25—26	Job 8
☐ January 13	Genesis 27—28	
☐ January 14	Genesis 29—30	Job 9

Date	Reading	Devotion
❑ January 15	Genesis 31—33	
❑ January 16	Genesis 34—35	Job 10
❑ January 17	Genesis 36—38	
❑ January 18	Genesis 39—40	Job 11
❑ January 19	Genesis 41—42	
❑ January 20	Genesis 43—45	Job 12
❑ January 21	Genesis 46—47	
❑ January 22	Genesis 48—50	Job 13
❑ January 23	Exodus 1—2	
❑ January 24	Exodus 3—4	Job 14
❑ January 25	Exodus 5—6	
❑ January 26	Exodus 7—8	Job 15
❑ January 27	Exodus 9—10	
❑ January 28	Exodus 11—12	Job 16
❑ January 29	Exodus 13—14	
❑ January 30	Exodus 15—16	Job 17
❑ January 31	Exodus 17—18	
❑ February 1	Exodus 19—21	Job 18
❑ February 2	Exodus 24	
❑ February 3	Exodus 32—35:3	Job 19
❑ February 4	Exodus 39:32—40	
❑ February 5	Leviticus 23; 25—27	Job 20
❑ February 6	Numbers 1:1-3; 8—10	
❑ February 7	Numbers 11—13	Job 21
❑ February 8	Numbers 14, 16	
❑ February 9	Numbers 17—18	Job 22
❑ February 10	Numbers 20—21	
❑ February 11	Numbers 22—23	Job 23
❑ February 12	Numbers 24—25	
❑ February 13	Numbers 27—29	Job 24
❑ February 14	Numbers 30—31	

Date	Reading	Devotion
☐ February 15	Numbers 32—33:1; 50—56	Job 25
☐ February 16	Numbers 35—36	
☐ February 17	Deuteronomy 1—3	Job 26
☐ February 18	Deuteronomy 4—5	
☐ February 19	Deuteronomy 6—8	Job 27
☐ February 20	Deuteronomy 9—10	
☐ February 21	Deuteronomy 11—12	Job 28
☐ February 22	Deuteronomy 13—15	
☐ February 23	Deuteronomy 16—17	Job 29
☐ February 24	Deuteronomy 18—19	
☐ February 25	Deuteronomy 26—27	Job 30
☐ February 26	Deuteronomy 28—29	
☐ February 27	Deuteronomy 30—32	Job 31
☐ February 28	Deuteronomy 33—34	
☐ March 1	Joshua 1—2	Job 32
☐ March 2	Joshua 3—4	
☐ March 3	Joshua 5—6	Job 33
☐ March 4	Joshua 7—9	
☐ March 5	Joshua 10—11	Job 34
☐ March 6	Joshua 12—13	
☐ March 7	Joshua 14—15	Job 35
☐ March 8	Joshua 16—17	
☐ March 9	Joshua 18—20	Job 36
☐ March 10	Joshua 21—22	
☐ March 11	Joshua 23—24	Job 37
☐ March 12	Judges 1—2	
☐ March 13	Judges 3—4	Job 38
☐ March 14	Judges 5—7	
☐ March 15	Judges 8—9	Job 39
☐ March 16	Judges 10—11	
☐ March 17	Judges 12—13	Job 40

Date	Reading	Devotion
☐ March 18	Judges 14—15	
☐ March 19	Judges 16—18	Job 41
☐ March 20	Judges 19—21	
☐ March 21	Ruth	Job 42
☐ March 22	1 Samuel 1—2	
☐ March 23	1 Samuel 3—4	Song of Songs 1
☐ March 24	1 Samuel 5—6	Song of Songs 2
☐ March 25	1 Samuel 7—8	Song of Songs 3
☐ March 26	1 Samuel 9—10	Song of Songs 4
☐ March 27	1 Samuel 11—12	Song of Songs 5
☐ March 28	1 Samuel 13—15	Song of Songs 6
☐ March 29	1 Samuel 16—17	Song of Songs 7
☐ March 30	1 Samuel 18—19	Song of Songs 8
☐ March 31	1 Samuel 20—21	Proverbs 1:1-19
☐ April 1	1 Samuel 22—23	Proverbs 1:20-33
☐ April 2	1 Samuel 24—26	Proverbs 2:1-9
☐ April 3	1 Samuel 27—28	Proverbs 2:10-22
☐ April 4	1 Samuel 29—31	Proverbs 3:1-18
☐ April 5	2 Samuel 1—2	Proverbs 3:19-35
☐ April 6	2 Samuel 3—4	Proverbs 4:1-13
☐ April 7	2 Samuel 5—6	Proverbs 4:14-27
☐ April 8	2 Samuel 7—8	Proverbs 5:1-14
☐ April 9	2 Samuel 9—10	Proverbs 5:15-23
☐ April 10	2 Samuel 11—12	Proverbs 6:1-19
☐ April 11	2 Samuel 13—14	Proverbs 6:20-35
☐ April 12	2 Samuel 15—17	Proverbs 7:1-5
☐ April 13	2 Samuel 18—19	Proverbs 7:6-27
☐ April 14	2 Samuel 20—21	Proverbs 8:1-21
☐ April 15	2 Samuel 22—24	Proverbs 8:22-36
☐ April 16	1 Kings 1—2	Proverbs 9:1-12
☐ April 17	1 Kings 3—4	Proverbs 9:13-18

Date	Reading	Devotion
❑ April 18	1 Kings 5—6	Proverbs 10:1-17
❑ April 19	1 Kings 7—9	Proverbs 10:18-32
❑ April 20	1 Kings 10—11	Proverbs 11:1-15
❑ April 21	1 Kings 12—13	Proverbs 11:16-31
❑ April 22	1 Kings 14—16	Proverbs 12:1-11
❑ April 23	1 Kings 17—18	Proverbs 12:12-28
❑ April 24	1 Kings 19—20	Proverbs 13:1-12
❑ April 25	1 Kings 21—22	Proverbs 13:13-25
❑ April 26	2 Kings 3—4	Proverbs 14:1-14
❑ April 27	2 Kings 5—6	Proverbs 14:15-35
❑ April 28	2 Kings 7—8	Proverbs 15:1-15
❑ April 29	2 Kings 9—10	Proverbs 15:16-33
❑ April 30	2 Kings 11—12	Proverbs 16:1-9
❑ May 1	2 Kings 13—15	Proverbs 16:10-33
❑ May 2	2 Kings 16—18	Proverbs 17:1-14
❑ May 3	2 Kings 19—20	Proverbs 17:15-28
❑ May 4	2 Kings 21—22	Proverbs 18:1-12
❑ May 5	2 Kings 23—24	Proverbs 18:13-24
❑ May 6	2 Kings 25; Obadiah	Proverbs 19:1-15
❑ May 7	Jonah	Proverbs 19:16-29
❑ May 8	Isaiah 1—3	Proverbs 20:1-15
❑ May 9	Isaiah 4—5	Proverbs 20:16-30
❑ May 10	Isaiah 6—8	Proverbs 21:1-15
❑ May 11	Isaiah 9—10	Proverbs 21:16-31
❑ May 12	Isaiah 11—12	Proverbs 22:1-16
❑ May 13	Isaiah 13—14	Proverbs 22:17-29
❑ May 14	Isaiah 15—16	Proverbs 23:1-21
❑ May 15	Isaiah 17—19	Proverbs 23:22-35
❑ May 16	Isaiah 20—21	Proverbs 24:1-22
❑ May 17	Isaiah 22—23	Proverbs 24:23-34
❑ May 18	Isaiah 24—25	Proverbs 25:1-13

Date	Reading	Devotion
❏ May 19	Isaiah 26—27	Proverbs 25:14-28
❏ May 20	Isaiah 28—30	Proverbs 26:1-12
❏ May 21	Isaiah 31—32	Proverbs 26:13-28
❏ May 22	Isaiah 33—34	Proverbs 27:1-22
❏ May 23	Isaiah 35—36	Proverbs 27:23-27
❏ May 24	Isaiah 37—38	Proverbs 28:1-14
❏ May 25	Isaiah 39—41	Proverbs 28:15-28
❏ May 26	Isaiah 42—43	Proverbs 29:1-14
❏ May 27	Isaiah 44—45	Proverbs 29:15-27
❏ May 28	Isaiah 46—47	Proverbs 30:1-17
❏ May 29	Isaiah 48—49	Proverbs 30:18-33
❏ May 30	Isaiah 50—52	Proverbs 31:1-9
❏ May 31	Isaiah 53—55	Proverbs 31:10-31
❏ June 1	Isaiah 56—57	Ecclesiastes 1:1-11
❏ June 2	Isaiah 58—59	Ecclesiastes 1:12-18
❏ June 3	Isaiah 60—61	Ecclesiastes 2:1-11
❏ June 4	Isaiah 62—63	Ecclesiastes 2:12-26
❏ June 5	Isaiah 64—66	Ecclesiastes 3:1-8
❏ June 6	Amos 1—3	Ecclesiastes 3:9-22
❏ June 7	Amos 4—5	Ecclesiastes 4:1-8
❏ June 8	Amos 6—7	Ecclesiastes 4:9-16
❏ June 9	Amos 8—9	Ecclesiastes 5:1-7
❏ June 10	Micah 1—3	Ecclesiastes 5:8-20
❏ June 11	Micah 4—5	Ecclesiastes 6:1-6
❏ June 12	Micah 6—7	Ecclesiastes 6:7-12
❏ June 13	Hosea 1—3	Ecclesiastes 7:1-14
❏ June 14	Hosea 4—5	Ecclesiastes 7:15-29
❏ June 15	Hosea 6—7	Ecclesiastes 8:1-9
❏ June 16	Hosea 8—9	Ecclesiastes 8:10-17
❏ June 17	Hosea 10—11	Ecclesiastes 9:1-12
❏ June 18	Hosea 12—14	Ecclesiastes 9:13-18

Date	Reading	Devotion
☐ June 19	Nahum	Ecclesiastes 10:1-10
☐ June 20	Zephaniah	Ecclesiastes 10:11-20
☐ June 21	Jeremiah 1—2	Ecclesiastes 11:1-8
☐ June 22	Jeremiah 3—4	Ecclesiastes 11:9-10
☐ June 23	Jeremiah 5—6	Ecclesiastes 12:1-8
☐ June 24	Jeremiah 7—8	Ecclesiastes 12:9-14
☐ June 25	Jeremiah 9—10	Psalm 1
☐ June 26	Jeremiah 11—12	Psalm 2
☐ June 27	Jeremiah 13—14	Psalm 3
☐ June 28	Jeremiah 15—16	Psalm 4
☐ June 29	Jeremiah 17—18	Psalm 5
☐ June 30	Jeremiah 19—20	Psalm 6
☐ July 1	Jeremiah 21—22	Psalm 7:1-8
☐ July 2	Jeremiah 23—24	Psalm 7:9-17
☐ July 3	Jeremiah 25—27	Psalm 8
☐ July 4	Jeremiah 28—29	Psalm 9:1-12
☐ July 5	Jeremiah 30—31	Psalm 9:13-20
☐ July 6	Jeremiah 32—33	Psalm 10:1-7
☐ July 7	Jeremiah 34—35	Psalm 10:8-18
☐ July 8	Jeremiah 36—38	Psalm 11
☐ July 9	Jeremiah 39—40	Psalm 12
☐ July 10	Jeremiah 41—42	Psalm 13
☐ July 11	Jeremiah 43—44	Psalm 14
☐ July 12	Jeremiah 45—46	Psalm 15
☐ July 13	Jeremiah 47—49	Psalm 16
☐ July 14	Jeremiah 50—52	Psalm 17:1-9
☐ July 15	Habakkuk 1—3	Psalm 17:10-15
☐ July 16	Lamentations 1—2	Psalm 18:1-12
☐ July 17	Lamentations 3—5	Psalm 18:13-34
☐ July 18	Ezekiel 1—2	Psalm 18:35-50
☐ July 19	Ezekiel 3—4	Psalm 19:1-6

Date	Reading	Devotion
☐ July 20	Ezekiel 5—6	Psalm 19:7-14
☐ July 21	Ezekiel 7—8	Psalm 20
☐ July 22	Ezekiel 9—10	Psalm 21
☐ July 23	Ezekiel 11—13	Psalm 22:1-11
☐ July 24	Ezekiel 14—15	Psalm 22:12-31
☐ July 25	Ezekiel 16—17	Psalm 23
☐ July 26	Ezekiel 18—19	Psalm 24
☐ July 27	Ezekiel 20—21	Psalm 25:1-7
☐ July 28	Ezekiel 22—23	Psalm 25:8-22
☐ July 29	Ezekiel 24—25	Psalm 26
☐ July 30	Ezekiel 26—27	Psalm 27:1-6
☐ July 31	Ezekiel 28—29	Psalm 27:7-14
☐ August 1	Ezekiel 30—32	Psalm 28
☐ August 2	Ezekiel 33—34	Psalm 29
☐ August 3	Ezekiel 35—36	Psalm 30
☐ August 4	Ezekiel 37—39	Psalm 31:1-18
☐ August 5	Ezekiel 40—42	Psalm 31:19-24
☐ August 6	Ezekiel 43:1-12; 47:1-12	Psalm 32
☐ August 7	Joel	Psalm 33:1-9
☐ August 8	Daniel 1—2	Psalm 33:10-22
☐ August 9	Daniel 3—5	Psalm 34:1-10
☐ August 10	Daniel 6—7	Psalm 34:11-22
☐ August 11	Daniel 8—9	Psalm 35:1-10
☐ August 12	Daniel 10—12	Psalm 35:11-28
☐ August 13	Ezra 1—2	Psalm 36
☐ August 14	Ezra 3—4	Psalm 37:1-11
☐ August 15	Ezra 5—6	Psalm 37:12-29
☐ August 16	Ezra 7—8	Psalm 37:30-40
☐ August 17	Ezra 9—10	Psalm 38:1-14
☐ August 18	Haggai	Psalm 38:15-22
☐ August 19	Zechariah 1—2	Psalm 39

Date	Reading	Devotion
☐ August 20	Zechariah 3—4	Psalm 40:1-10
☐ August 21	Zechariah 5—6	Psalm 40:11-17
☐ August 22	Zechariah 7—8	Psalm 41
☐ August 23	Zechariah 9—10	Psalm 42
☐ August 24	Zechariah 11—12	Psalm 43
☐ August 25	Zechariah 13—14	Psalm 44:1-8
☐ August 26	Esther 1—3	Psalm 44:9-26
☐ August 27	Esther 4—5	Psalm 45:1-9
☐ August 28	Esther 6—8	Psalm 45:10-17
☐ August 29	Esther 9—10	Psalm 46
☐ August 30	Nehemiah 1—2	Psalm 47
☐ August 31	Nehemiah 3—4	Psalm 48
☐ September 1	Nehemiah 5—7:5	Psalm 49
☐ September 2	Nehemiah 8—10	Psalm 50:1-15
☐ September 3	Nehemiah 12:27—13:31	Psalm 50:16-23
☐ September 4	Malachi 1—2	Psalm 51
☐ September 5	Malachi 3—4	Psalm 52
☐ September 6	Matthew 1—3	Psalm 53
☐ September 7	Matthew 4—5	Psalm 54
☐ September 8	Matthew 6—8	Psalm 55:1-15
☐ September 9	Matthew 9—10	Psalm 55:16-23
☐ September 10	Matthew 11—12	Psalm 56
☐ September 11	Matthew 13—16	Psalm 57
☐ September 12	Matthew 17—18	Psalm 58
☐ September 13	Matthew 19—20	Psalm 59
☐ September 14	Matthew 21—23	Psalm 60
☐ September 15	Matthew 24—25	Psalm 61
☐ September 16	Matthew 26—28	Psalm 62
☐ September 17	Mark 1—2	Psalm 63
☐ September 18	Mark 3—4	Psalm 64
☐ September 19	Mark 5—6	Psalm 65

Date	Reading	Devotion
☐ September 20	Mark 7—8	Psalm 66
☐ September 21	Mark 9—10	Psalm 67
☐ September 22	Mark 11—12	Psalm 68:1-18
☐ September 23	Mark 13—14	Psalm 68:19-35
☐ September 24	Mark 15—16	Psalm 69:1-15
☐ September 25	Luke 1—3	Psalm 69:16-36
☐ September 26	Luke 4—5	Psalm 70
☐ September 27	Luke 6—7	Psalm 71:1-11
☐ September 28	Luke 8—9	Psalm 71:12-24
☐ September 29	Luke 10—11	Psalm 72
☐ September 30	Luke 12—14	Psalm 73:1-17
☐ October 1	Luke 15—16	Psalm 73:18-28
☐ October 2	Luke 17—18	Psalm 74
☐ October 3	Luke 19—20	Psalm 75
☐ October 4	Luke 21—22	Psalm 76
☐ October 5	Luke 23—24	Psalm 77
☐ October 6	John 1—3	Psalm 78:1-31
☐ October 7	John 4—6	Psalm 78:32-55
☐ October 8	John 7—8	Psalm 78:56-72
☐ October 9	John 9—11	Psalm 79
☐ October 10	John 12—13	Psalm 80
☐ October 11	John 14—16	Psalm 81
☐ October 12	John 17—18	Psalm 82
☐ October 13	John 19—21	Psalm 83
☐ October 14	Acts 1—2	Psalm 84
☐ October 15	Acts 3—4	Psalm 85
☐ October 16	Acts 5—6	Psalm 86
☐ October 17	Acts 7—8	Psalm 87
☐ October 18	Acts 9—10	Psalm 88
☐ October 19	Acts 11—13	Psalm 89:1-18
☐ October 20	Acts 14—15	Psalm 89:19-45

Date	Reading	Devotion
☐ October 21	Acts 16—17	Psalm 89:46-52
☐ October 22	Acts 18—19	Psalm 90
☐ October 23	Acts 20—21	Psalm 91
☐ October 24	Acts 22—24	Psalm 92
☐ October 25	Acts 25—26	Psalm 93
☐ October 26	Acts 27—28	Psalm 94:1-11
☐ October 27	James 1—2	Psalm 94:12-23
☐ October 28	James 3—5	Psalm 95
☐ October 29	Galatians 1—2	Psalm 96
☐ October 30	Galatians 3—4	Psalm 97
☐ October 31	Galatians 5—6	Psalm 98
☐ November 1	1 Thessalonians 1—2	Psalm 99
☐ November 2	1 Thessalonians 3—5	Psalm 100
☐ November 3	2 Thessalonians 1—3	Psalm 101
☐ November 4	1 Corinthians 1—2	Psalm 102
☐ November 5	1 Corinthians 3—4	Psalm 103
☐ November 6	1 Corinthians 5—7	Psalm 104
☐ November 7	1 Corinthians 8—9	Psalm 105:1-22
☐ November 8	1 Corinthians 10—11	Psalm 105:23-45
☐ November 9	1 Corinthians 12—13	Psalm 106:1-5
☐ November 10	1 Corinthians 14—16	Psalm 106:6-48
☐ November 11	2 Corinthians 1—2	Psalm 107:1-22
☐ November 12	2 Corinthians 3—5	Psalm 107:23-43
☐ November 13	2 Corinthians 6—7	Psalm 108
☐ November 14	2 Corinthians 8—9	Psalm 109:1-20
☐ November 15	2 Corinthians 10—11	Psalm 109:21-31
☐ November 16	2 Corinthians 12—13	Psalm 110
☐ November 17	Romans 1—3	Psalm 111
☐ November 18	Romans 4—5	Psalm 112
☐ November 19	Romans 6—7	Psalm 113
☐ November 20	Romans 8—9	Psalm 114

Date	Reading	Devotion
☐ November 21	Romans 10–11	Psalm 115
☐ November 22	Romans 12–14	Psalm 116
☐ November 23	Romans 15–16	Psalm 117
☐ November 24	Colossians 1–2	Psalm 118
☐ November 25	Colossians 3–4	Psalm 119:1-32
☐ November 26	Philemon	Psalm 119:23-56
☐ November 27	Ephesians 1–3	Psalm 119:57-88
☐ November 28	Ephesians 4–6	Psalm 119:89-112
☐ November 29	Philippians 1–3	Psalm 119:113-144
☐ November 30	Philippians 4–6	Psalm 119:145-176
☐ December 1	1 Timothy 1–2	Psalm 120
☐ December 2	1 Timothy 3–4	Psalm 121
☐ December 3	1 Timothy 5–6	Psalm 122
☐ December 4	Titus	Psalm 123
☐ December 5	1 Peter 1–2	Psalm 124
☐ December 6	1 Peter 3–5	Psalm 125
☐ December 7	Hebrews 1–2	Psalm 126
☐ December 8	Hebrews 3–4	Psalm 127
☐ December 9	Hebrews 5–6	Psalm 128
☐ December 10	Hebrews 7–8	Psalm 129
☐ December 11	Hebrews 9–10	Psalm 130
☐ December 12	Hebrews 11–13	Psalm 131
☐ December 13	2 Timothy 1–2	Psalm 132
☐ December 14	2 Timothy 3–4	Psalm 133
☐ December 15	2 Peter	Psalm 134
☐ December 16	Jude	Psalm 135
☐ December 17	1 John 1–3	Psalm 136
☐ December 18	1 John 4–5	Psalm 137
☐ December 19	2 John	Psalm 138
☐ December 20	3 John	Psalm 139
☐ December 21	Revelation 1–2	Psalm 140

Date	Reading	Devotion
☐ December 22	Revelation 3—4	Psalm 141
☐ December 23	Revelation 5—6	Psalm 142
☐ December 24	Revelation 7—8	Psalm 143
☐ December 25	Revelation 9—10	Psalm 144
☐ December 26	Revelation 11—12	Psalm 145
☐ December 27	Revelation 13—14	Psalm 146
☐ December 28	Revelation 15—16	Psalm 147
☐ December 29	Revelation 17—18	Psalm 148
☐ December 30	Revelation 19—20	Psalm 149
☐ December 31	Revelation 21—22	Psalm 150

Endnotes

1. Oprah Winfrey, quoted on "Inspirational Quotes: Wisdom Quotations." www.inspirational-quotations.com/wisdom-quotes.html (accessed December 2005).
2. Holly Wagner, *GodChicks* (Nashville, TN: Thomas Nelson Publishers, 2003), p. 29.
3. James Strong, *The New Strong's Exhaustive Concordance of the Bible* (Nashville, TN: Thomas Nelson Publishers, 1990), Hebrew #2428.
4. Valerie Monroe, "Age Brilliantly, Beautifully, Happily," *O, The Oprah Magazine*, October 2005.
5. Wagner, *GodChicks*, p. 70.
6. Ibid., p. 75.
7. Ibid., p. 107.
8. Carl Rogers, quoted in James Hewitt, ed., *Illustrations Unlimited* (Wheaton, IL: Tyndale House, 1988), p. 388.
9. Terri Apter and Ruthellen Josselson, *Best Friends* (New York: Three Rivers Press, 1999), p. 198.
10. Jim Burns, "The Ultimate Christmas Present," *Devotions on the Run* (Ventura, CA: Regal Books, 2004), Week 3/Sunday reading.
11. *Guideposts* Magazine (Carmel, NY: December 1989), p. 28, quoted in Burns, "The Ultimate Christmas Present," *Devotions on the Run*, Week 3/Sunday reading.
12. Ibid.
13. Hewitt, ed., *Illustrations Unlimited*, p. 224.
14. Ibid, p. 445.

Thanks

To Jesus . . . for making life
such an adventure!

To my Oasis family . . . for praying
for me so much this year.

To Philip . . . for loving me every day.

To Paris and Jordan . . . for providing me
with lots of illustrations!

To Ashley . . . for the typing, the
encouragement and the words.

Inspiring Reading
for Women

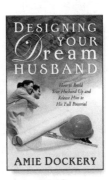
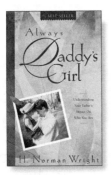

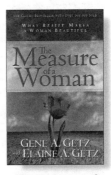

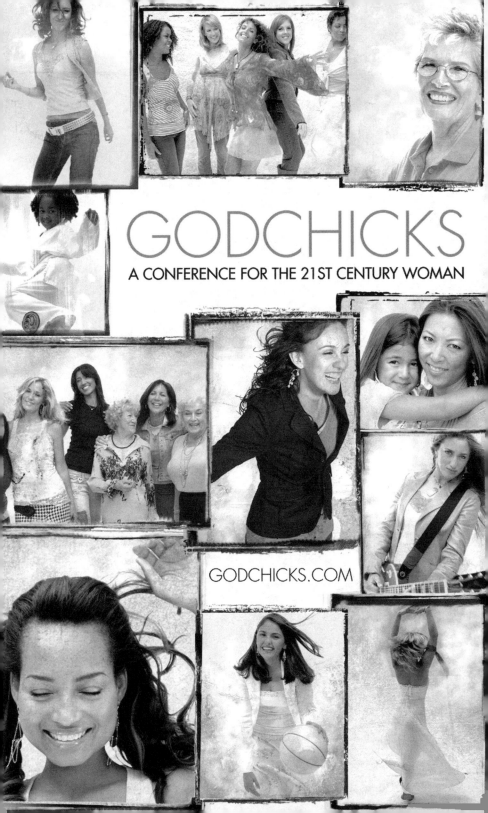

GODCHICKS

A CONFERENCE FOR THE 21ST CENTURY WOMAN

GODCHICKS.COM